RUSSIA / IN / REVOLUTION

Бронштейнъ Лейба Давидовъ

1 22

HARRISON E. SALISBURY

RUSSIA IN REVOLUTION 1900-1930

DESIGNED BY JEAN-CLAUDE SUARES

ANDRE DEUTSCH
WILLIAM COLLINS (Canada)

First published 1978 by
André Deutsch Limited
105 Great Russell Street London WC1

Printed in Great Britain by
GPS (Print) Limited, London

British Library Cataloguing in Publication Data

Salisbury, Harrison Evans
    Russia in revolution, 1900-1930.
    1. Russia – History – 20th century
    I. Title
    947.08   DK246

    ISBN 0 233 97013 4

Assistant Designer: Sam Woo
Photo Research: J-C Suarès, Emily Blain Chewning
Permissions: Emily Blain Chewning, Boylston Tomkins
Production: Sam Woo, Susan Willmouth, Ken Kleppert
This edition published in association with
William Collins Sons & Co. Canada Ltd.,
100 Lessmill Road, Don Mills, Ontario, Canada.

ACKNOWLEDGEMENTS

The author, editors and publishers would like to thank the following for their kind permission to reproduce material which appears on the pages noted.

A La Vieille Russie, Inc, New York: 9, 16 (T & B), 20-21, 29, 56 (TL), 57, 71, 73 (T), 79, 88, 89.

Associated Press: 286-287

Camera Press: 3, 100-101, 127, 170-171.

Ex Libris, New York: 155, 189, 190, 250 (L), 278 (R), 279, 285.

Malcolm Forbes Collection, New York: 11, 14-15, 23 (T & B), 44-45.

Galerie Jean Chauvelin, Paris: 187.

Collection of George Gibbes, London: 13, 19, 180.

The Solomon R. Guggenheim Museum, New York: 46, 47, 48-49, 50 197.

The Hoover Institution, Stanford, California: 24 (all), 25, 26, 27 (both), 66 (B), 107 (both), 110, 120-121, 148, 150-151, 153, 154, 156-157, 230, 231, 247.

Robert Hunt Library, London: 94-95.

Imperial War Museum, England: 85, 106, 174, 246.

Keystone: 224-225, 266 (TL), 266 (B), 270.

Life Picture Service: 269.

Musée de Bale, Switzerland: 196 (TL), 196 (B).

The Museum of Modern Art, New York: 193, 243.

The Museum of Modern Art Film/Stills Collection, New York: 252, 252-253, 254 (both), 255 (both), 256, 257, 258-259.

The Museum of Modern Art Gravure Collection, New York; Gift of Phillip Johnson: 277.

The New York Public Library Picture Collection: 10 (B), 18 (R), 30, 33, 34, 35, 36 (R), 37, 42-43, 61 (L), 61 (TR), 64 (T), 68, 69, 83, 97, 99 (L), 104, 109, 114, 123, 125, 141, 165, 184-185, 194, 195, 201, 211 (B), 214 (T & B), 233, 244 (all), 249 (B), 261, 263, 271, 283, 284 (BL & BR).

Novosti Agency: 245.

Radio Times Hulton Picture Library, London: 181.

Roger-Viollet, Paris: 36 (L), 67, 84, 90-91, 102, 104-105.

Russian Literature Tri-Quarterly, (©) 1976 by Ardis: 249 (T), 250 (R).

Sotheby Parke Bernet & Co., London: 60 (T).

Sofoto: 2.

Staatsbibliothek, Berlin: 76-77.

Stedelijk Museum, Amsterdam: 248.

Tass: 272-273.

Tretyakov Gallery, USSR: Endpapers and Cover.

United Press International, New York archives: 4, 28, 38-39, 73 (B), 74-75, 78 (T & B), 80 (T & B), 81 (T & B), 86-87, 93, 103, 111, 113, 115, 126, 128, 130-131, 135, 136, 137, 138-139, 144, 147, 160-161, 167, 172-173, 175, 176-177, 196 (TR), 209, 212-213, 215, 216-217, 221, 222 (both), 223, 228, 229, 235, 238, 239, 266 (TR), 274-275, 280-281, 284 (T).

USIS, Paris: 117, 162, 168.

Wadsworth Atheneum, Hartford, Connecticut: 65.

Thomas P. Whitney Collection, Connecticut: 40-41, 54 (all), 55, 58 (B), 59, 66 (T), 129, 133, 146 (both), 159, 169 (both), 179, 183 (both), 188, 191, 192 (T & B), 207, 208, 211 (T), 219, 226, 227, 236-237, 241, 251 (all), 265, 267, 268, 282.

Images on the following pages are from sources which do not wish to be identified:
10 (T), 12 (T & B), 18 (L), 22, 51, 56 (TL & TR), 58 (T), 60 (B), 61 (BR), 62-63, 64 (B), 98, 99 (TR & BR), 100, 112, 119, 124, 134, 143, 145, 149, 163, 202, 203, 204-205, 240, 262, 278 (L).

CHAPTER 1

Coronation mugs passed out at Khodinka field in Moscow on the occasion of Nicholas II's coronation in 1896. Hundreds of people were killed in a panic touched off by the distribution, an event which many superstitious Russians felt was an omen foretelling the tragedy of the Romanovs.

Nicholas and Alexandra in a portrait taken April 18, 1894 outside the chapel at Coburg, Germany after the ceremony marking their engagement to marry.

One of Nicholas II favorite recreations was canoeing. Here he is with his canoe in the Gulf of Finland off Tsarskoye Selo.

FACING PAGE
Imperial banner, especially woven in silk for the coronation ceremonies of Nicholas II in 1896.

The sea was like glass. By the day the sun shone with summer warmth and at night there was a touch of autumn chill. Czar Nicholas II was enjoying himself enormously, surrounded by all his family including his beloved year-old son, Alexis, his "treasure", heir to the throne of all the Russias. The time was September 1905. It had been a dreadful year. The war with Japan had started badly and ended in disaster. And on the terrible day of January 9, 1905, when tens of thousands of workers and their families led by the priest, Father Gapon, had marched on Palace Square in St Petersburg, begging to submit a petition to the Czar, hundreds had been mowed down by Cossack fire. Bloody Sunday was the name under which it went down in history. The foundations of the Russian Empire seemed to shake. Disorder spread across the country.

The Czar could hardly bear to recall this but now he thought it lay behind him. Peace had been signed with Japan at Portsmouth, New Hampshire, through the mediation of Theodore Roosevelt, a better peace than might have been expected, and the Czar had made concessions which he felt should satisfy his restless peoples. If not, first-class troops would soon be returning from the Far East to put down any further outbreaks. He was convinced that the threat of Revolution had receded.

The Czar relaxed. He liked nothing in the world so much as the sea. Once aboard the Imperial yacht, *Polar Star,* with its mahogany doors and cabin fittings, its brass hardware, the familiar Captain Fabritsky and his friendly crew, the escort of naval vessels, it was hard to believe that the Japanese had sent most of Russia's fleet to the bottom and that Bloody Sunday might be an augury for the future.

Each afternoon the yacht anchored off one of the islands in the Baltic sea with its cover of birch and pine, bilberry bogs and blueberry patches. The Imperial party put ashore. There were picnics from wicker baskets, the food spread over snowy linen, the Imperial princesses in sailor hats and sailor suits with blue-striped sailor jerseys, sometimes (but not always) accompanied by the beautiful Czarina Alexandra and her new-found friend, Anna Vyrubova, making up a gay company. They hunted for mushrooms, picked berries and explored paths into the woods. Two or three beaters thrashed through the underbrush, stirring up game for the Czar and his companions; not very serious hunting, but the Czar enjoyed it. His score for the expedition was six grouse (he missed two shots), one raven, four rabbits, one big fox, a woodpecker, and a seagull. Other members of the party shot a dozen rabbits, a pair of grouse, two owls and a crow.

Two or three times on starlit nights there were fireworks for the children and by day the Czar took his daughters rowing in a small boat. The Czarina and Madame Vyrubova played duets on the piano. They adored Beethoven and Tchaikovsky and delighted in their new friendship. The Czar was pleased that little Alexis seemed to love the sea. Already the Czar and the Czarina knew that the child suffered from hemophilia but on this voyage Alexis was well and healthy. Everyone got tanned and the sun peppered little bridges of freckles across the noses of the fair-skinned girls. In

Nicholas and his son Alexis photographed in ordinary Russian military dress.

The daughters of Nicholas II and Alexandra were beautiful, particularly the oldest girls, the Grand Duchesses Olga and Tatiana. The Grand Duchess Marie lacked the statuesque quality of her older sisters. Anastasia was a madcap.

FACING PAGE
Nicholas II loved exercise. He never missed his daily walk, sometimes he rode a bicycle.

Not all the elaborate Fabergé eggs were made for the Imperial family. This golden egg with crimson enamel, rose and table-cut diamonds, was presented by the exceedingly wealthy Alexander Kelch, an owner of Siberian gold mines, to his wife in 1898.

Grand Duke Michael, heir-apparent to the Russian throne, and Grand Duchess Olga, brother and sister of Nicholas II, in 1895.

Czarina Alexandra Feodorovna and a lady-in-waiting with two pages on swings. Swinging was a traditional Russian woman's recreation.

FACING PAGE TOP
Grand Duke Constantine, uncle of Czar Nicholas II, and his family.

FACING PAGE BOTTOM
Left to right: Nicholas II and Alexandra Feodorovna, Grand Duchesses Olga and Zenia, sisters of Nicholas II, Grand Duke Michael (grand-uncle of Nicholas II) and Grand Duke Alexander, first cousin of Nicholas II. Taken about 1900.

the evenings the Czar read to his family. They went to bed early. Vyrubova sometimes fell asleep while drinking her bedtime tea. The Czar had left the cares of duty behind but he did receive his great statesman, Serge Witte, who had signed the Portsmouth treaty. He congratulated Witte and made him a count.

"I am happy as a child in this liberty and peace," the Czar wrote his mother, "and above all with this life on the water."

When the Czar returned to St Petersburg on September 18 he could see but a single cloud on the sunny horizon and this had nothing to do with war or social unrest. The Czar's cousin, the Grand Duke Kyril Vladimirovich, had provoked a scandal by marrying the Grand Duchess Victoria Fedorovna, divorced wife of the Czarina's brother. Nicholas had warned Kyril against this gross breach of protocol. Now Kyril had not only married the divorcee but had brought her to the capital. The Czar was exceedingly angry. He ordered Kyril out of Russia, removed his name from the ranks of the armed forces, deprived him of royal subsidies and took away his title of Grand Duke. Later he relented and let Kyril keep his title.

"Ouf!" he wrote his mother. "What worrying and disagreeable days!"

It gave him a headache. But now it was over. All was well with his Empire and he could devote himself to the celebration of the Czarevich's name day, October 5.

All was well? All was well with this enormous empire of 120,000,000 people, its sixty nationalities (not for nothing was Russia known as "the prisonhouse of peoples"), its expanse which encompassed a dozen time zones from the Duchy of Poland to Vladivostok? The Czar might with greater realism have concluded that *nothing* was well with the kingdom which he still ruled as a total autocracy.

For a century the realm had been stirring. The Russian officers who marched down the Champs Elysée with Alexander I after defeating Napoleon had brought back into the slumbering empire the deadly virus of change. They had tasted the fruits of growing freedom in western, industrializing Europe and they wanted to lead their backward homeland into the nineteenth century or — at least the eighteenth.

And so the struggle had started. On the side of change, one generation of idealistic, liberal young people after another. Against them, the stalwart, unbending Imperial autocracy. There had been a flurry of hope in the 1860's when Alexander II succeeded his father, Nicholas I, "Iron Nicholas". Alexander had ended serfdom, relaxed the grim hold of the police over his subjects and introduced a whiff of enlightenment.

But that had not lasted long and it all went down the drain when the frustrated young radicals known as the People's Will succeeded in assassinating the Czar himself

Czarevich Alexis, heir to the throne of Russia, wears a military uniform and boots as he plays with his dog.

RIGHT
Nicholas II loved to relax in informal settings. Shortly after ascending the throne he takes his ease in a villa outside Petersburg. On the wall are portraits of his family. One of the Czarina is just above his head.

FACING PAGE
The Grand Duchesses Tatiana and Olga in the uniforms of the Guards regiments of which they were honorary colonels.

on March 1, 1881, blowing him up by the banks of the Catherine Canal in St Petersburg.

All was well in the Czar's Empire? Only four years earlier the *Samara Gazette* published a small story. Nothing elaborate. It told of the death of an eighteen-year-old teacher in a village school of the Novgorod guberniya. The girl's name was A.M. Yeremeyeva. Her life did not differ from that of many village teachers, that is, she was paid at below-subsistence level. She got seven-and-a-half rubles a month, about $4 at the prevailing rate of exchange. Her tiny room cost three rubles a month. She had four-and-a-half rubles left for food and clothing. Her story was quite unexceptional — except that the authorities forgot to pay her for two months and, as a result, she starved to death.

As a delegate to a Moscow teacher's convention in 1902 pointed out, another 11,000 rural school teachers existed on the edge of starvation. Many lived in huts with the peasants' cattle. Many were housed in unheated sheds. Most of them simply squatted in a corner of a single-room schoolhouse.

There is no evidence that Czar Nicholas II had any knowledge of Yeremeyeva's plight nor was this an incident so exceptional that it attracted much attention. Starvation was perhaps not a way of life in the Czar's Russia. But it was familiar enough.

Just ten years earlier the rich and productive lands of the middle Volga had been swept by one of the worst famines of the century. Tens of thousands of peasants died of hunger and of epidemic diseases like cholera. The famine raged for more than two years. The tragedy aroused the anger, indignation and emotion of Russian intellectuals, led by Leo Tolstoy, who went to the Volga and set up an emergency program to feed the starving.

The Imperial government was encouraging the export of grain to finance railroad building and did its best to suppress news of the disaster. "In Russia," it announced, "there is no famine. But there are localities suffering from a failure of crops."

To which Tolstoy replied:

The common people are hungry because we are too full. All our palaces, all our theaters, museums, all this stuff, these riches of ours we owe to the effort of these same hungry people who make these things. This means that they will always be obliged to do this kind of work to save themselves from the death by starvation that constantly hangs over their heads.

On November 3, 1895 the
Grand Duchess Olga
Nikolayevna, first child of
Nicholas II and his wife
Alexandra, was born. The
St Petersburg nobility
presented this Fabergé icon to
the Imperial couple depicting
their patron saints and the
four Evangelists.

Until early in this century barges on Russian rivers were often pulled by men or women. Here peasant women pull a barge along the Sura River.

22

This was the verdict not of some young revolutionary but of Russia's great philosopher-writer, a towering figure in the world. As for the radicals, the Volga and Tambov famines were grist for their mill; mounting evidence of the rottenness of the Imperial system; its inability, indeed its refusal, to cope with the social and economic problems that wracked the nation, the chronic phenomenon of starvation amidst plenty, of skin-and-bones amid ermines and sables, of gaunt beggars, magnificent palaces, diseased children, expensive jewels, mass illiteracy and the greatest luxury the world had ever seen.

In October, 1905, Nicholas was thirty-seven years old and had reigned for eleven years. Despite the tiny concessions which he had made in August 1905, his power was even more absolute than that of Michael Romanov, first of the line elected to the throne in 1613 by the Moscow boyars.

Alone among the ruling heads of Europe, the Czar wielded total authority. No parliament curbed him. No popular elections. No courts. The press was censored and suppressed at his will. His ministers might advise but his was the last word. Nicholas was the supreme autocrat. He had no intention of yielding his power, nor would his firm-willed wife, Alexandra, have agreed even had he so wished.

Russia was Europe's largest and most backward nation. But what no one understood, not the Czar, not most of his advisors, not many of his subjects, still 95 percent illiterate and little more than a generation removed from serfdom, nor the other European powers, was that the industrial revolution which had swept England, France and Germany in the 1830's had now seized Russia. She was rushing hell bent into the new age of iron and steam engines, building railroads faster than America, expanding her steel industry at a dizzying rate, developing oil fields, textile mills, machine tool plants, banks and commerce at a pace that would give her first place in the world — if catastrophe did not overwhelm her in the next twenty or thirty years.

The onset of industrialization was shaking the lives of the "black people", as the peasants called themselves, the silent masses who perpetually walked with backs bent from heavy burdens, their gait slow and plodding from years of pulling at ploughs, sledges or barges, the people of the Russian steppe which reached to the far horizon like an earthen sea. It was a land where the people lived by the belief that the Czar was distant and the heavens high, where men of God in greasy brown robes and bark shoes wandered, sustained by bowls of food offered by people who had not a kopek to their name.

Now these peasants were beginning to throng into the cities, finding jobs in burgeoning textile plants, lodgings in dirty wooden barracks, wages of a handful of kopeks a day — a pittance but still more than they could earn in the new farms being organized by wealthy landlords and greedy middle-farmers, the men they called *kulaks*. Kulak means "fist" in Russian. It was with their stone-hard fists that the kulaks beat their way up from grinding poverty.

Nowhere in the world was there a revolutionary tradition so fierce as Russia's — born in the deadly dialectic of force and counter-force. One generation after another had tried to change Czarist despotism and, finding that reason, persuasion and propaganda simply sent them to the gallows or hard-labor exile in Siberia, turned to violence.

Russia was the home of anarchism, of the doctrine that destruction is creative, that only blood can purify the land, of "the worse the better" (a terrible philosophy which led some radicals of the 1890's, including Vladimir Lenin, to argue it was better to let the peasants starve than feed them, because thus their hatred for the Czar would be strengthened and the day of the autocrat's downfall be brought closer).

The People's Will had been wiped out by the police after their assassination of Alexander II. But new revolutionaries sprang up in their place. Lenin's older brother, Alexander, and four of his classmates at St Petersburg University were hanged for an adolescent plot to kill Alexander III in 1887. But not all plots were abortive, and as Russia moved into the twentieth century more and more high officials of the Czar's regime fell victim to terror; two successive Ministers of the Interior, one of them V. K. Plehve, the Czar's "strong man"; a Minister of Education; the Czar's Uncle, the Grand Duke Sergei Alexandrovich; Prime Minister Peter A. Stolypin; high officials of the police, the governor-general of Finland, and dozens of others.

Типы Россіи. — Types de Russie. 25

МОСКВА. — MOSCOU.

№ 10

Благовѣщенскій Соборъ въ Кремлѣ. — Cathédrale de l'Annonciation au Kremlin. 225

A mother in a slum quarter of St Petersburg instructs her daughter in the alphabet, using an advertisement for a concert of Russian music as a text.

RIGHT
A street vendor sells oddments. Most of his stock is thread and yarn.

Mother and daughter shopping, tins for milk and kerosene.

RIGHT
Peasant woman selling pencils and shoelaces.

Street vendor selling leather.

RIGHT
Street vendor with his stock of scarves and knitted goods draped around his shoulders.

FACING PAGE
A Russian coachman about 1900. They were noted for their bulk and ability to consume unlimited quantities of vodka.

In the years before the
Revolution Russia was
thronged with wanderers who
made their way from village
to village living on food and
alms given by the peasants.

FACING PAGE TOP
Siberian women in holiday
dress.

FACING PAGE
BOTTOM
Village elders sit for a
portrait. Their wives take
second place.

СВ. МУЧЕНИКЪ АЛЕЗАНДРЪ

Peasants offer food for sale in the Moscow Streets.

Icon painting is the most ancient of Russian arts. It flourished until the 1917 Revolution. This icon of St Alexander the Martyr is a handsome example of modern icon-making. It is signed by Gourianov and dated 1910.

Most of these victims of revolutionary terror were killed by what was called the "Fighting Arm" of the Socialist Revolutionary Party which took up the banner of terror from the broken People's Will group. The Socialist Revolutionaries led by Viktor Chernov came to be the most feared of all the revolutionaries so far as Czar Nicholas and his advisors were concerned. The SR's stood uncompromisingly for terror and they won the support of millions of peasants with the doctrine that only the peasants should possess Russia's land.

Russia's Marxist movement was less prominent in the early 1900's than it would be later. It had arisen in large measure out of despair — the despair of young people and intellectuals that terror alone would not smash the Empire. Karl Marx proclaimed that the downfall of capitalism was inevitable; that the proletariat was certain to inherit the earth. To many turn-of-the-century Russian revolutionaries these were comforting words. Marx gave them the conviction that they would win in the end despite the immense forces which the Czar mustered against them.

By 1905 there were no less than three Marxist groups in Russia, all describing themselves as Social Democrats. The most radical was headed by Vladimir Ulyanov, that is Lenin. Lenin, son of a Volga river school inspector, had been an active revolutionary for more than ten years and was now based in exile in Switzerland, refuge of many of the revolutionaries. His group was called Bolshevik, or majority, because they had won a majority in a Social Democratic Congress in London in 1903. His principal opponents among the Social Democrats took the name Menshevik (minority). They had been the minority group at London. Junius Martov (formerly a close friend and associate of Lenin's) was their principal leader. The Mensheviks stood for revolution, just as did Lenin's Bolsheviks, but they believed in a more democratic, more open Party. Lenin founded his group on conspiracy, underground work in Russia, iron discipline and tight direction closely held in his hands. The third group of Marxists were the "legalists". They believed in reform not Revolution. They concentrated on applying Marxist principles to analyzing economic and social problems.

Apart from the Social Revolutionaries and the Social Democrats, there was one other great revolutionary group — the anarchists. They derived their philosophy from the gentle and idealistic Prince Peter Kropotkin, and believed in the total destruction of all ruling states and systems and a society in which no man had authority over any other man. As to how this might be brought about, they were largely incoherent. But on one thing they agreed. The first step was the extermination of the Czarist system by violent, unrestrained terror.

A bit to the right but also committed to basic political change was the group which soon coalesced under the banner of the Constitutional Democratic Party — the Kadets — in Russian usage. They believed in a constitutional monarchy similar to that of England in which a parliament ruled in the name of a titular monarch.

While the revolutionary and Marxist parties were small in numbers they had great sympathy among the ranks of Russia's educated citizenry, the so-called intelligentsia. Generation after generation of young people of Russia had been attracted to this cause, led by idealistic sentiments and dreams of freedom and a principled relationship of man to man, stimulated by Russia's great writers, beginning with the poet, Pushkin, and coming down to Turgenev and Tolstoy. The intelligentsia was activated by a profound belief that Russia's despotic monarchism was morally and socially rotten. As the years passed more and more felt that only by destruction of the whole system and its replacement by a new socially-conscious society could the ills be cured.

FACING PAGE
On Sunday, January 9, 1905 Father Gapon, head of a workers' society sponsored by the Czar's secret police, led thousands of St Petersburg workers to the Winter Palace. The workers carried religious banners and portraits of the Czar and the Czarina and sought to present a petition to Nicholas II, telling of their life and hardships and praying for his help. Instead regiments of the Imperial guards opened fire. Hundreds were killed. Bloody Sunday touched off the first Russian Revolution — that of 1905.

CHAPTER 2

Caricatures drove home the point that the Czarist government had drowned the 1905 Revolution in blood.

By 1906 the Revolution had been crushed and Russia lay wounded and stunned while the Czar's punitive military detachments swept through city and countryside shooting and hanging those accounted guilty of defying the Government. This 1906 issue of the Satirical Review (the magazines changed names and titles almost monthly as they were suppressed by the Czarist censors) depicts fallen Russia attacked by human vipers.

FACING PAGE
The Revolution of 1905 came to its climax in December in the streets of Moscow where government troops smashed an effort by the revolutionaries to take over power. This woman worker carrying a banner enscribed 'Freedom' is surrounded by a wall of bayonets.

The Czar's respite was brief. He had hardly returned to St Petersburg before the repercussions of Bloody Sunday became apparent. The level of violence began to rise in the Russian countryside. Arson — the "red cock" — stalked the vast estates as sullen and angry peasants put the torch to the barns and manor houses of the landowners. Sometimes, friendly peasants warned the proprietors, even apologized, but nonetheless burned the houses to the ground. "We're sorry but we have no choice," the peasants said. They did not explain why they had no choice. To many it seemed that mania was sweeping across the steppes, grim and without remorse. By mid-October Russia was in chaos. Strikes boiled up in St Petersburg and Moscow. Railroads all over the country ground to a halt. Connections to the Far Eastern armies were broken. Not a wheel turned in the Russian capital. Even ballet dancers and bank clerks quit their jobs. The Czar's generals issued proclamations, but dared not call on the troops to restore order. A Soviet — a council — of Workers and Peasants sprang into being. One of its leaders was a man named Bronstein, then going under the *nom de guerre* of Yanovsky. Later he became better known as Leon Trotsky.

Trotsky was almost unique among the Russian revolutionaries who for three generations had been trying to change Russia. At the first word of Bloody Sunday he hastened to return to St Petersburg from exile in Switzerland. The other leaders of the revolutionary sects — Georgi V. Plekhanov, Martov, Chernov, Lenin, Catherine Breshko-Breshkovskaya (the little grandmother of the Russian Revolution, as she was known) and Pavel Milyukov, leader of the soon-to-be-formed Kadet Party, elected to stay abroad — in Switzerland, the United States, France, wherever they happened to be. Like the Czar they did not really believe the Empire could be falling apart. After all they had no hand in the events of Bloody Sunday and little enough in what followed.

By October 17, 1905 the Czar found himself almost a prisoner in his palace at Tsarskoye Selo on the Gulf of Finland, twenty miles outside St Petersburg. He no longer dared come into the city to the Winter Palace. His ministers travelled back and forth by dispatch boat. The trains had stopped running. Not a few believed the fall of the Czarist system was at hand. Count Witte gave the Czar an ultimatum; either proclaim a parliament (Duma) with general elections and himself, Witte, at the head of the government or turn matters over to the army to crush the revolution in blood. The Czarina dissolved into hysterics. The Czar turned to his most reliable military advisor, General Trepov. Trepov recommended acceptance of Witte's proposals rather than a bloodbath. The Czarina and the Czar's courtiers fought to the last against a parliament. But on the morning of October 17 Grand Duke Nikolai Nikolaevich, "Nikolasha," the Czar's cousin, a magnificent man who stood nearly six foot eight, appeared at Tsarskoye Selo. He had a Browning pistol in his pocket and warned that he would shoot himself if the Czar failed to proclaim the Duma.

The Czar yielded. The proclamation was posted on the walls of the city. St Petersburg and Moscow erupted in demonstrations. Everyone took to the streets — Grand Dukes, princesses, the singer Chaliapin, Maxim Gorky, the ballerinas, working men, their wives, the bewildered revolutionaries, angry bands of "black hundreds" (reactionary anti-semitic groups). They sang and marched and shouted and sometimes clashed. Russia had never seen anything like it. The absolute tyranny of the old Romanov rule had come to an end.

The Czar hardly knew what he had done. He wrote his mother:

> There was no way out but to make the sign of the cross and do what the world demanded. The only consolation is the hope that through the bounty of God this difficult decision will help Russia to emerge from untenable chaos. We find ourselves in the midst of a revolution.....I know that you pray for your poor Nicky. May Christ be with you. God will save and calm Russia.

Three more weeks were to pass before Lenin, later to be hailed as the supreme revolutionary tactician, arrived back in Russia. He thought that he was putting himself at the head of the Revolution. But already the flames of revolt were being smothered by punitive expeditions set in motion by the Czar and his military commanders. They

КАРИКАТУРНЫЙ ЛИСТОКЪ ГАЗЕТЫ ГАЗЕТЪ

Leon Trotsky as a young student in his native Nikolayev, a shipbuilding center on the Black Sea.

RIGHT
Jewish victim of a pogrom at Belostok.

FACING PAGE
This cartoon shows the Czar's ministers preparing to decorate the Tauride Palace, seat of the Government, with human skulls.

OVERLEAF
Life in Russian villages did not materially improve after the Revolution. In most of the countryside there was
36 *sharp deterioration.*

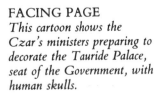

marched through the countryside, killing and hanging and burning the peasant huts. Savage pogroms touched off by the Czar's secret police ravaged Kiev, Odessa and Kishinev. The cry: *Bei zhidov!* 'Beat the Jews!' rang through Russia's streets. Hundreds of Jews were killed, their shops burned and pillaged. The Czar brushed aside protests. A thousand people died when a theater was set afire in the old Siberian city of Tomsk.

When the revolutionaries, at Lenin's call, sought in December to set the revolt going again with a general strike in Moscow the Czar rushed in his crack Semenovsky Guards. The troops relentlessly shelled the workers' stronghold in the Presna district, destroying factories and burning tenements. By December 19 it was all over. There were a thousand casualties, dead and wounded. But the violence went on. In Latvia peasants burned nearly half the thousand estates of the landlords. The Czar's troops retaliated by destroying 300 peasant villages, hanging and shooting at random. Between 1905 and 1907 2,000 estates were ravaged in Russia in 2,600 peasant outbreaks. For months peasants were executed in batches of 20 or 25, 160 in one week, often a hundred or more a month. In the autumn of 1905 alone casualties were estimated at 4,000 killed, 10,000 wounded, many of them in the terrible pogroms. No one knows how many deaths there were in all, possibly 30,000 or 40,000. Millions of Jews left the country in an epic migration that brought many to the shores of the United States.

Lenin and some of his fellow revolutionaries stayed on in Russia and Finland (then part of the Empire), trying to fan the embers of revolt. But the moment had passed.

To the Czar, to Russia's politicians, to the revolutionaries, and to the peasants, the years after 1905 stretched out grim and banal. To the revolutionaries, dispersed once more in Switzerland, Austria, Paris, New York or exile in Siberia, the spark of unrest seemed to have been extinguished by the blood shed in the *karatelny* or punitive expeditions which so ravaged the countryside that Leo Tolstoy exploded in a pamphlet, *I Cannot be Silent:* "It is impossible to live so....Either these inhuman deeds may be stopped or my connection with them may be snapped and I put in prison where I may be clearly conscious that these horrors are not committed on my behalf."

Despite Tolstoy the reprisals moved forward inexorably under the firm hand of Premier Stolypin, the ablest man the Czar was ever to select as his first minister. Stolypin was aware of the danger posed to Russia by the contrast between the backwardness and illiteracy of her peasantry and booming industrialization. He embarked on a breakneck program to create a new class of small farmers, able peasants, owning their own farms, hiring labor, utilizing the latest in equipment and agricultural techniques; a substitute for the traditional "black people" working on the immense

Boris M. Kustodiev
commemorated the 1905
Revolution with this peasant
striding over the old symbols of
Russia.

Some caricaturists saw the 1905
Revolution as a skeleton
haunting the Russian scene.

Czarist troops drawn up in Palace Square ready to open fire on demonstrators, 9 January, 1905.

Nathalia Goncharova and Mikhail Larionov worked so closely over the years it is almost impossible to speak of one without the other. They moved through almost every phase of the Russian avant garde. Goncharova's Cats, *painted in 1913, belongs to their Rayonist period.*

latifunda (some of a million acres or more) which were still in the hands of a few hundred extraordinarily rich nobility.

Stolypin hoped to save Russia from disaster by erecting a middle class which would create the efficient agriculture and industry necessary if Russia was to take a place in the forefront of European powers. Together with a handful of emerging Russian entrepreneurs — men like the St Petersburg steel king and banker, Putilov, and the progressive Moscow multimillionaires, the Morozovs, the Ryabushinskys, and the railroad magnate, Savva Mamontov — Stolypin understood that Russia was in a race against time. Either the medieval structure of the state must be changed within the decade or internal contradictions would destroy it.

The steel magnate Putilov was convinced that Russia was headed for mindless revolt and anarchy. His predictions were more dramatic and, as it proved, more accurate than those of the Russian revolutionaries, so torn with factional strife and dialectical arguments that they had little conception of what was happening in their homeland.

The revolution in art had been long brewing. Like everything in the Czar's domain, art had been dominated, controlled and financed by the State. Russian art had been born out of the subventions and directives of Catherine the Great, who founded the Russian Academy of Art in 1764. The State financed the training of artists. The State selected those worthy of development. The State drafted the curriculum of the Academy, picked the professors, specified the style and subject of paintings and sculpture (neo-classical). The State and the court were the principal consumers of the products of painters and sculptors, buying their works for the Imperial collections.

And the State carefully monitored its artists. It maintained an official known as a *politsmeister* in the Academy whose functions were precisely those which the name suggests, that is to keep order and enforce discipline among aspiring students. Study abroad was discouraged or permitted most grudgingly.

But the turbulence in Russian life which marked the latter half of the nineteenth century could not leave the world of art untouched. New, revolutionary movements

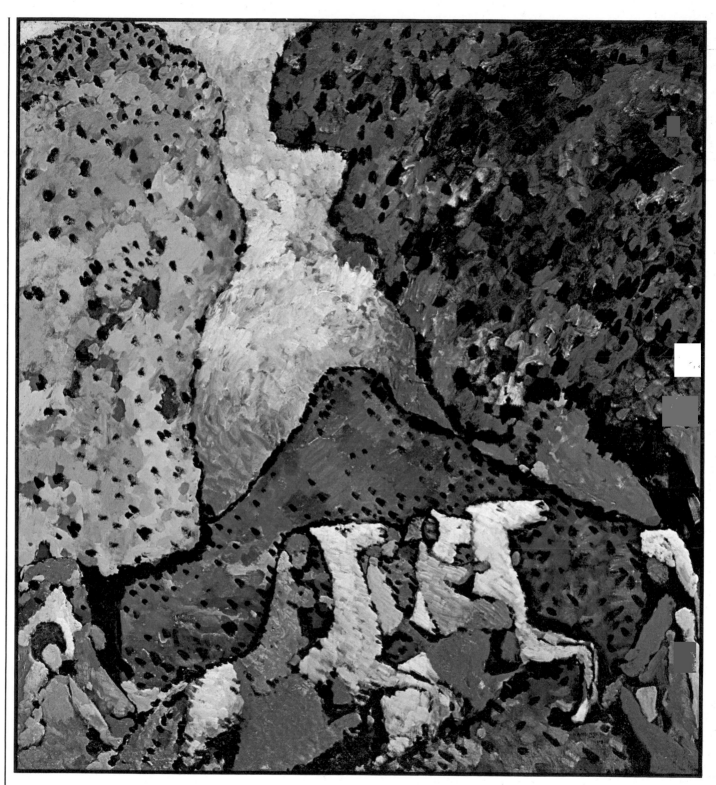

sprang up — the Wanderers, dedicated to painting the reality of Russian life and stirring the social consciousness of the Russian people. Ilya Repin, Viktor Vasnetsov, Vasily Surikov, Vasily Perov and Konstantin and Vladimir Makovsky, Wanderers all, sent their paintings on annual tours throughout Russia and finally toppled the official school. By 1900 the Wanderers had themselves become the establishment and a new, wildly imaginative generation was carrying the revolution forward.

The assault of the new generation fell upon every aspect of the arts — painting, music, drama, poetry, the dance. It was supported and financed by an extraordinarily wealthy generation of patrons. Pavel Tretyakov, founder of the famous museum that still bears his name in Moscow (he gave it to the city in the 1890's), helped support the

Vasily Kandinsky worked in Munich rather than in Paris where so many of his Russian colleagues congregated. His first Russian exhibition was in Odessa together with the Burliuks, Larionov, Goncharova and Exter. This painting is Blue Mountain, No 84, *dated 1908.*

Vasily Kandinsky's work is closely related to the World of Art movement in Russia and particularly to World of Art poets like Andrei Bely. This is Study for Composition II, 1909-10.

new painting. So did the immensely wealthy Kiev sugar family of Tereshchenko. But even greater contributions came from the rich railroad magnate, Savva Mamontov, whose estate at Abramtsevo became a fusion point for Russian art, music and literature, nurturing such talents as those of Levitan, Korovin, Vasnetsov, Rimsky-Korsakov, Serov, Nikolai Roerich and ultimately the incomparable Sergei Diaghilev, founder of modern ballet, and Mikhail Vrubel, sometimes confined to a madhouse.

Another remarkable patron, Savva Morozov, a textile heir, financed both revolutionary politicians (including Lenin) and revolutionary creators. It was his money that enabled Konstantin Stanislavsky and Vladimir Nemirovich-Danchenko to found the Moscow Art Theater. Savva's cousin, Ivan Morozov, accumulated the greatest Russian collection of Matisse and exquisite examples of Cezanne, Monet, Gauguin and Renoir. His collection and the even more impressive one of his fellow Moscow millionaire, Ivan Shchukin, were rich in works by Matisse, Picasso, Cezanne, Manet, Monet, Degas and Renoir. These collections influenced the Russian avant garde — Malevich, Goncharova, Larionov, Tatlin, Sudeikin, Rosanova, Popova, Mashkov, Lissitsky, Kusnetsov, Konchalovsky, Kliun, Kandinsky, Filonov, Falk, Chagall, Benois, Bakst and Altman. It was hard to tell where to draw the line between the art of Paris and that of Russia. In fact there were so many Cezannes in Moscow collections that he was known as "our own Russian artist".

In those years when political revolution was dead in Russia these men and women carried out a revolution in taste, style and standards which still makes the mind whirl.

In this milieu poets agonized in a world of illusion that sometimes slipped over into madness. Valery Bryusov created an apocalyptic vision of the 1905 Revolution two years before it occurred. Andrei Bely, a friend and rival poet, wrote a novel, *The Silver Dove*, which he later realized pre-figured peasant violence, 1917 and the savaging of

Natalia Goncharova supported Larionov's Rayonist creed of 1911: "We declare the genius of our days to be: trousers, jackets, shoes, tramways, buses, aeroplanes, railways, magnificent ships....." in The Cyclist *of 1912-13 she conveys her preoccupation with machines, speed, brilliant colors.*

Russia's intelligentsia. The poets and painters gathered in the quarters of the mystic philosopher Vyacheslav Ivanov and debated questions of good and evil, virtue and lust, and particularly the principle of salvation through sin, a principle already being advocated by a still rather obscure *strannik*, a wandering holy man, named Grigory Rasputin, just beginning a career as seducer of society women and soon to become confidante to the Imperial family, the man whom Nicholas and Alexandra would credit with saving the life of the hemophilic Czarevich and whom history would give a central role in the Romanov disaster.

In poetry, in art, in music nothing now seemed impossible. Russia was dissolving in tragedy but never had art been more brilliant. It was noontide for the Moscow Art theater with Stanislavsky presenting Chekhov's *The Seagull, The Cherry Orchard,* and *Uncle Vanya,* Maxim Gorky's *The Lower Depths,* Maeterlinck's *The Bluebird* and the dark tragedies of Strindberg and Andreyev. Nothing like Stanislavsky's realism had been seen on the stage and the Czar feared that *The Lower Depths* would undermine the Empire, so faithfully did Gorky present the horror of Russian life.

The extinction of the Revolution of 1905 had no effect on the revolution in Russian art. Kasimir Malevich, then aged 27, arrived in Moscow simultaneously with the December uprising. First, he distributed revolutionary literature then turned back to painting and rapidly developed the Cubo-Futuristic style, characteristic of his Morning in the Country After a Snowstorm, *1912.*

51

CHAPTER 3

At Easter 1911, the fifteenth anniversary of his accession to the throne, Nicholas II presented this egg to Czarina Alexandra Feodorovna. The egg is made of gold and enamelled white, with garlands of green enamel, and decorated with diamonds. Inset are ivory miniatures of the coronation and other commemorative scenes as well as portraits of Nicholas and Alexandra and the date 1911.

*The first – and for many
years the only – American
post-Revolutionary showing
of Russian art was held at
the Grand Central Palace in
New York in 1924. The
poster for the exhibition was
done by Boris Mikhailovich
Kustodiev.*

RIGHT
*No Russian artist so
effectively captured the rich,
lush self-satisfaction of the
pre-revolutionary merchant
class as did Boris
Mikhailovich Kustodiev.
Kustodiev, a man of infinite
talent, is hardly known
outside his own country. He
was a remarkable product of
the turn of the century. He
studied in St Petersburg,
Paris, Spain and Italy before
returning to Russia at the
time of the 1905 Revolution.
In* Beauty *he personifies and
satirizes the fleshly tastes of
the Russian merchant class.*

BELOW
*Kustodiev paints the well-
known pre-Revolutionary art
collector, F. F. Notgaft.*

FACING PAGE
The kupechestvo, *the
vigorous, hard-fisted Russian
merchant class, was one of
the principal targets of the
Revolution. Kustodiev's art
chronicled their sturdy
devotion to money and
possessions. Here a merchant,
surrounded by paper and
silver rubles, tallies up his
accounts on a wooden abacus.*

Authentic to the last detail —
a hardstone carving of a
peasant woman by Fabergé.

RIGHT
These are photographs of the
Moscow workshops of
Fabergé located on
Kuznetsky Most. Carl
Fabergé's sons, Eugene,
Agathon, Alexander and
Nicholas, often assisted their
father in designing works of
art.

Possibly the most exquisite of
the Fabergé creations were
the flower sprays. This one
is composed of cornflowers in
translucent enamel with rose
diamond centers, yellow gold
stalks and leaves, oats in red
gold and Chinese forget-me-
nots in turquoise with rose
diamond centers and yellow
gold stalks and leaves.

FACING PAGE
The Orange Tree Egg by
Fabergé was presented by
Nicholas II to his mother,
the Dowager Empress Marie
Feodorovna, in 1911. It is
based on a block of nephrite
on which is set a white
quartz tub, set with cabochon
rubies and pearls. A gold tree
trunk supports egg-shaped
foliage of nephrite leaves
among which are set enamel
flowers with diamond centers
and topaz, amethyst, pale
rubies and champagne
diamond fruits. When a
button is pressed a feathered
gold bird arises from the
center of the tree, sings
briefly, and automatically
disappears.

Serge Diaghilev, about 1909.

Mikhail Larionov sketches himself, Sergei Prokofiev and Diaghilev at a rehearsal of Les Ballets Russes' production of Chout *in 1921.*

here was a feverish cast to the painted cheeks of Russian society. It was a time of extremes. The finest jewelry craftsmen in the world assembled in St Petersburg to cater to the whims of the Imperial family and the incredibly wealthy Russian aristocracy. Under the mark of Fabergé these skilled artists created magical baubles – sapphire cornflowers, ruby scarletinas, pearl-and-emerald lilies-of-the-valley, nosegays of precious stones whose sparkle blinded the viewer. Their supreme achievements, the Easter "surprises", were invented for the Imperial family. Each Easter the Czar (beginning with Alexander III and continuing through Nicholas II) presented a Fabergé egg to his wife. Such an egg! It might encase a miniature brood of chicks. Or it might harbor within an intricate gold-and-enamel shell a working replica of the Trans-Siberian railroad. Never had such costly, such elaborate, such entrancing objects of art been created. The Imperial family's patronage was worth several king's ransoms to the court jewelers. (The Empress Alexandra liked to shop around for bargains at lesser jewelers. But nothing could hurt the custom of Fabergé.)

Even Fabergé paled before the quintessence of Russian art – Diaghilev's opera and ballet. All of the revolutionary forces in Russian culture combined in the remarkable dancing of Nijinsky (later to go mad in Switzerland), the decor and painting of Bakst and Roerich (who went on to found a mystic cult), the unparalleled voice of that mountain of a man, Feodor Chaliapin, the fairytale eloquence of the premiere ballerinas Karsavina and Pavlova, the choreography of Fokine, the music of Rimsky-Korsakov, Borodin and Mussorgsky. Diaghilev brought an exhibition of Russian painting to Paris in 1907. In 1908 he brought the St Petersburg Opera. And on May 19,

Caricature of Diaghilev and his circle by Mikhail Larionov. About 1920.

Natalie Goncharova's sketches for Les Noces *for Les Ballets Russes, 1923.*

Nijinsky with his wife, the former Romola de Pulszka, and daughter on shipboard.

Vaslav Nijinsky in La Spectre de la Rose.

Serge Diaghilev and Nijinsky. A caricature by Jean Cocteau.

*The Bolshevik Revolution
did not — immediately — halt
the fervid evolution of
Russian art. But it began to
disperse it. Many Russian
artists went to Germany or
France. Diaghilev and Les
Ballets Russes went to Paris.
Jean Cocteau draws Igor
Stravinsky playing* The
Rites of Spring.

1913

1909 the Russian ballet opened at the Théâtre Châtelet. Neither Paris nor St Petersburg was ever to be the same again. Theater, dance, music, art was transformed. The synthesis of Russian theme and talent created a new world, the like of which no one in the West (or East) had ever seen. This *was* the Future. The Czar might still sit soddenly on his throne, Russian politicians might argue, peasants toil, workers sink into exhaustion, revolutionaries drown in debate and futility. But a new world had been born and its vision would echo through the corridors of the century, its resonance reverberating into our own times.

In Russian society it was an epoch of alienation. A decade earlier the heroes and heroines of young Russia had been the Decembrists, the young officers of noble families who had staged a demonstration in Senate Square in St Petersburg in 1826 at the time Nicholas I ascended the throne. Nicholas hanged a half dozen ringleaders and exiled the remainder to the desolate mines of eastern Siberia. The young wives accompanied their husbands to these remote regions.

Generations of Russians had worshipped at the shrine of the Decembrists and had hoped through noble deeds, heroism and acts of terror to advance the cause of freedom.

Now such goals seemed fatuous.

Young people turned to drink, to scandals, gambling, drugs and sexual license. Boris Azef, a police spy who infiltrated the Socialist Revolutionary terrorist section, where he simultaneously plotted assassinations of Grand Dukes and exposed to the police those who carried them out, became a symbol of the era — rootless, ambivalent, hypocritical. Smart St Petersburg society frequented gypsy restaurants. New nightclubs sprung up in the suburbs of the northern capital.

It was not the moral works of Tolstoy or Dostoyevsky, but a novel called *Sanin* by Artsybshev which matched the spirit of the times. Sanin, hero of the novel, is a monster of self-indulgence. Whatever his whim it must be satisfied. He subjugates women, twists them as he pleases and casts them off, often pregnant, sometimes to suicidal death. Only satisfaction matters. Such moral laxity was anathema to the Czar. But he was quite incapable of inspiring his countrymen. He was a modest good-hearted man. No one who knew him failed to remark on his pleasant manner. But few failed also to remark that intellect was not his strength. Even his Grand Ducal cousins

APRES MIDI D'UN FAUNE
(NIJINSKY)

BAKST

This photograph of Rasputin with the Czarina, Tsarevich Alexis and the Grand Duchess Marie circulated widely after February 1917. Rasputin sometimes spent the whole day with the Czarina and the children.

BELOW
The relationship of Rasputin with the Czar and the Czarina was subjected to savage caricature. Here they are shown as puppets of the monk.

FACING PAGE
Rasputin established close relations with the court entourage. Here he is pictured with Prince Poutiatine and Colonel Loman of the Palace Mixed Guard.

referred to him in private as "the Colonel". They thought he had the mentality of an ordinary Guards Colonel and this assessment, interestingly, was used later on by Trotsky. The Czar was born on May 6, the day celebrated by the Orthodox Church as the birthday of Job. He called himself a modern Job and seemed to feel that things never would go right for him. He loved his family, adored his wife and with the passage of years fell more and more under the influence of her dynamic will.

Superstition and spiritualism were much in vogue in St Petersburg. The Imperial family did its share of dabbling; despite the Czarina's English background she was a superstitious woman; mysticism and a belief in miraculous happenings ran deep in the house of Hesse. Her conversion to the Russian Orthodox faith at the time of her marriage to the Czar in 1894 strengthened her mystic bent as she came to believe in the oldest, most Orthodox strain of the Russian faith, replete with special prayers for special saints. The Czar did not follow his wife's example but he, too, had a tendency towards mysticism.

Very early on the Imperial couple had been attracted to a charlatan named Dr Philippe Vachot, a Frenchman who promised to help the Czarina bear an heir to the throne — a matter of some concern after she had born her fourth successive daughter, Anastasia, in 1902. Vachot was dismissed after the Czarina went through a false pregnancy. But he prophesied that "another friend" would make his appearance and he gave the Czarina a little bell. He promised it would ward off false advisors. The Czarina cherished the bell for the rest of her life and often reminded the Czar of its powers.

By the time Rasputin appeared, the professed "man of God" with powers which seemed to enable him to heal or mitigate the difficult, dangerous and painful attacks which beset the little Czarevich, the ground was well prepared.

Rasputin was introduced to the Imperial couple by two of the Grand Duchesses who had already become his converts. His influence with the Czar and Czarina grew rapidly in the years after 1905. He was, in fact, a simple but clever peasant from the forests of western Siberia. Like many peasants he had no family name. "Rasputin" was a nickname meaning "dissolute" and he won it by his easy conduct in his village where it was reputed that he had possessed almost every woman in the community, young and old. He had a wife and three children, two daughters and one mentally retarded son. His wife refused to be disturbed by Rasputin's conduct. "It makes no difference," she said, "he has enough for all."

As 1905 faded into the past, confidence returned to the Czar. He cut back on his promises of political reform. His great worry and that of the Czarina now lay with the health and well being of the Czarevich Alexis. With Rasputin's help the Imperial couple felt more secure in their private world where Alexandra and Nicholas customarily spoke and wrote (rather ungrammatical) English to each other. He called her "Sunny" or "Sunshine" and she called him "Dovey", "Hubby" or any one of a score of tender nicknames.

In those years poets like David Burliuk and Vladimir Mayakovsky wandered the countryside dressed in yellow waistcoats with radishes in their boutonnieres, scrawling obscenities on their faces in white chalk, reciting verses and shocking the citizenry. It was a time for breaking icons and tearing down idols. Nothing was sacred to the new generation. The Czar's censors banned their works. Sometimes they were threatened with jail (official Russia has never been hospitable to new talent and new ideas) but they thumbed their noses and went ahead with new brawls and new scandals. Some went mad. When World War I broke out the poet Andrei Bely thought it was evil forces within himself which had unleashed the armies. Suicide was not uncommon. Two young women poets in love with a third poet, Valery Bryusov, successively took their own lives. Both Bely and Bryusov came close to suicide several times.

There is no indication that the Czar noticed any of this. Nor, so far as their writing indicates, did any of the leaders of the revolutionary factions, scribbling busily away for their tiny journals and pamphlets in dismal back-floor bedrooms in Geneva and Paris.

At 9 pm on the evening of September 1, 1911 two pistol shots rang out in the magnificent Kiev Opera House, crowded with dignitaries attending a special performance

of *The Tale of Czar Sultan* by Rimsky-Korsakov. It was being presented on the occasion of a visit by Czar Nicholas II.

The Czar was unhurt. The target was his prime minister, Stolypin. The wounds proved fatal and within four days he was dead. His assassin was a police stoolpigeon and informer named Bogrov and to this day suspicion persists that in some fashion the police were implicated in the murder. Earlier he had come to the police with vague and confused stories about an assassination attempt, and it was the police who provided Bogrov with his ticket of admission.

Stolypin was the most important of a series of victims whose deaths were attributable to the interrelationship between the secret police, revolutionary organizations and unstable, unreliable elements in the population.

Since medieval times the Russian Czars had founded their rule on secret police and police terror. Ivan the Terrible's dread *Oprichniki* had set the pattern. The names changed with the changes of rulers and the passage of centuries but the principles remained the same. Nicholas I, "Iron Nicholas" who came to the throne in 1825, had his "Third Section". It penetrated every level of Russian society with spies, informers and secret agents. Every line of matter printed in Russia passed through the hands of the censors and every letter going in and out of the country was steamed open and read by a "black chamber". Under Nicholas II the secret police were known as the *Okhrana* but their tactics were identical to those of their predecessors. The intricate relationship between police and revolutionaries had been growing over the years. Father Gapon, the worker priest who led the fateful demonstration before the Winter Palace on January 9, 1905 headed a workers' organization which had been established and inspired by the police. Boris Azef, the SR terrorist, had been a police informer before he joined the SR fighting squad. Police undercover agents had a hand in the assassinations of the Grand Duke Sergei and Interior Minister Plehve. Police agents infiltrated all the Revolutionary parties. Often the agents hardly knew in which capacity they were acting – police spy or revolutionary terrorist. Within three years of Stolypin's death the leading Bolshevik spokesman, Malinovsky, head of the Bolshevik faction in the Duma, would be exposed as "Agent X" of the Czar's secret police. When Malinovsky spoke in the Duma his speech was sometimes written by the police, sometimes by Lenin, sometimes by both.

Nowhere was the putrefaction of Russian society more striking than in this symbiosis of the two great enemies, the forces of Government, of Law and Order and those of Change, Revolution and Destruction.

Neither the Czar nor the Czarina grieved over Stolypin's death nor (apparently) gave much heed to the fact that he had been killed by a police spy. Much more important to both was the fact that Stolypin was an enemy of Rasputin and Rasputin was now the strongest single influence upon the Czarina and, through her, a growing influence upon the Czar.

Father Gapon, leader of the January 9, 1905 demonstration at the Winter Palace in St Petersburg, was "executed" eighteen months later in a Finnish summer house, charged by SR revolutionaries with being a traitor. Here his body is laid out for a postmortem.

CHAPTER 4

This poster appeals for aid for Russian prisoners of war in World War I.

The Czar chose Count V. N. Kokovtsev as Stolypin's successor. He was a man of integrity but without the energy and statesmanship needed to cope with the storm rising over Europe. The great powers were engaged in a deadly minuet. Russia and England had long been rivals. France was Russia's ally. Emperor Wilhelm II, "Cousin Willy" to Nicholas' "Cousin Nicky", had been trying for years through letters, flattery, cajolery and trickery to get Russia to line up with Germany (and her ally Austria-Hungary) in support of Wilhelm's boundless ambition. Gradually a German-English rivalry had begun to supplant the traditional Anglo-Russian conflict.

Now through cautious and skilful diplomacy by the French and particularly by England's Lord Grey, Russia was moving into a Triple Entente which was balanced against the German–Austrian alliance. Every statesman in Europe knew that positions were being taken up which would be likely to lead to general European war. The British and German navies were racing to head each other off. The French and German General staffs matched each other's preparations step-for-step. Only Russia lagged. Her arms industry was not yet large enough to support her mass army, her railroad network was incapable of carrying the burden of full mobilization as well as industrial and grain traffic, her bureaucracy was lumbering and archaic, her peasants were rude and illiterate, her social system was at odds with itself, her leadership was weak and uncertain. It was a recipe for disaster. Premier Kokovtsev warned the Czar that Russia was dangerously unprepared and that the War Minister, General Sukhomlinov, was incompetent. The Czar did nothing.

For the first time since 1905 industrial strife emerged on the home front. Workers in the British-owned goldfields on the remote Arctic Lena river went on strike in April 1912. The gendarmes opened fire and shot down more than a hundred. This touched off a wave of strikes, two-thirds of them political, which persisted to the eve of War.

Despite stress in Europe and strain within Russia the year 1913 seemed to augur well for the Czar and his regime. It was the 300th anniversary of the dynasty. The Imperial family made a pilgrimage across the country to every ancient city and place connected with the founding of the dynasty – to Vladimir, once the capital of Russia, to Suzdal, city of ancient cathedrals, to the village of Bogolubov where the Romanovs had their obscure beginnings, to Nizhni Novgorod (now Gorky), the magnificent trade city on the Volga, to Kostroma and Yaroslavl, to Rostov Veliki and to Moscow.

It was a pilgrimage of triumph. Everywhere the Czarevich, a beautiful, strong boy despite his hereditary illness, was carried through the ceremonies in the strong arms of a sailor companion. Alexis had suffered a critical attack of hemophilia in the autumn of 1912 when the family was visiting in Poland. The court physicians lost hope for the child's life as he lay in agony in a hunting lodge at Spala. But Rasputin telegraphed from Siberia: "The illness is not as dangerous as it seems. Don't let the doctors worry him."

From this moment forward Alexis began to improve. He was not completely recovered by the time of the celebrations but well enough to participate with his father and mother. Nicholas looked handsome in his uniforms. Alexandra showed the mark of years and worry. The four Imperial princesses won the hearts of every audience, dressed in long gowns of traditional Russian design.

Ancestors of Ivan Susanin, hero of Glinka's opera, the peasant who "gave his life for the Czar," were ferretted out, presented to the Czar and awarded state decorations. No one reminded the Czar of the grim words of Stolypin's widow, at the bedside of her martyred husband: "Ivan Susanin will not again come to Rus!"

In early 1914 Kokovtsev delivered a final warning to the Czar of the inevitability of war with Germany. The Czar silently stared into the distance and then muttered: "All is in the will of God." A few days later he discharged Kokovtsev and replaced him with the first of a series of mediocrities. The Czar's mother, the Dowager Empress Maria Feodorovna, sought to rouse her son to the perils of his course. She got nowhere. Peter Durnovo, a staunch and reactionary supporter of the dynasty, wrote the Czar that war with Germany would almost certainly lead to defeat and defeat would lead to "social revolution in its most extreme form". Durnovo's memorandum was found among the Czar's papers in 1917. Whether he read it is not known. That he did not act upon it is certain.

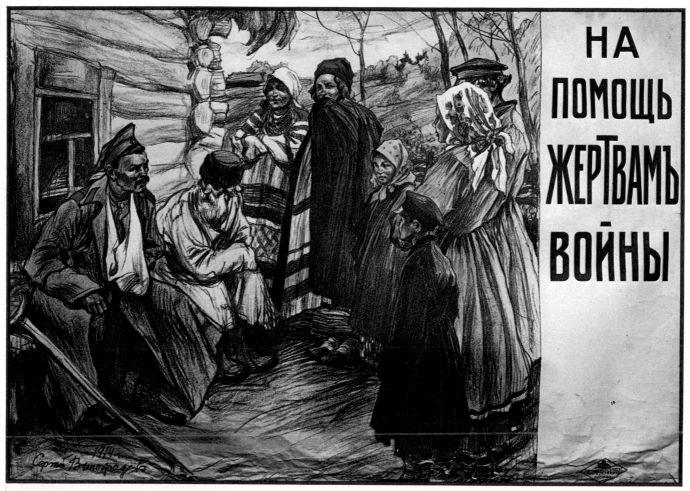

НА
ПОМОЩЬ
ЖЕРТВАМЪ
ВОЙНЫ

Nicholas II felt that he was in his element when war broke out. All his life he had a fondness for the military. Now he donned his uniform and almost daily inspected troops going up to the front.

PREVIOUS PAGE
A Cossack charge against the Germans in World War I.

Hundreds of thousands of Russian soldiers were taken prisoner in the huge offensive and defensive operations of the early phase of the war. These Russians are being marched across the German border under guard.

FACING PAGE
Colossal losses of men and arms on the German front compelled the Czarist government to turn more and more to large scale war loans. This poster calls for subscriptions to $5\frac{1}{2}$ percent war bonds.

The evening of Saturday July 12, 1914 was warm and pleasant at Krasnoye Selo, the formal military camp not far from the Czar's palace at Tsarskoye Selo. Krasnoye Selo was still decorated with the flags and banners which had been put up for the visit of President Poincaré of France who had just left aboard the battleship *France* after a state visit to Russia.

The visit had been a great success – fetes, military reviews, naval spectacles, state dinners, lavish entertainment and long diplomatic consultations. There had been a state dinner at the magnificent Peterhof, the Russian palace on the Gulf of Finland which rivalled Versailles (and where the Czar and Czarina never lived – they found it too lavish). The Czarina loathed public occasions but she had stayed at her husband's side throughout. Sixty thousand crack Russian troops paraded before Poincaré and the Imperial couple.

It had been a buoyant celebration, designed to demonstrate the unity of France and Russia and to nudge the British closer to full alliance. Not a single disagreement, the French ambassador Paléologue recalled, troubled the French and the Russians. The British Ambassador, Sir George Buchanan, was not so ebullient. He didn't think *all* the differences between Russia and England had yet been ironed out.

There was, however, a cloud in the sky – a simmering crisis over the assassination of the Austrian Archduke at Sarajevo three weeks earlier. The subsequent diplomatic row between Serbia and Austria had dragged on. The Austrian ambassador had suddenly returned to St Petersburg. Paléologue was afraid the crisis might escalate. He was pleased that the Czar and Poincaré seemed to see eye to eye – in case the trouble grew worse.

That evening the atmosphere at Krasnoye Selo was relaxed. Princess Cantacuzene, daughter of President Grant, whose husband was one of the officers on duty, looked forward to a pleasant evening. The Mariinsky ballet was performing in the pretty little camp theater. Soon after the Cantacuzenes took their places the Czar appeared with his aides, headed by the Grand Duke Nikolai Nikolaevich, commander of the Imperial Guard and of the camp. There was a rattle of sabres and spurs as the officers seated themselves. The Czar seemed at ease and happy.

The curtain rose and the performance began. Toward the end of the first act Princess Cantacuzene's sharp eyes caught the figure of Foreign Minister Sazonov quietly slipping into his seat. It was most unusual for a cabinet minister to be late for an Imperial performance. When the curtain went down the Czar had a few moments of conversation with Sazonov then ordered his limousine brought up and left the theater with his senior aides. Most of the audience left too. The news Sazonov had brought to the Czar was of an ultimatum from Austria to Serbia.

That night the Czar issued orders for preliminary mobilization. The camp at Tsarskoye Selo was broken up. The first steps toward putting the creaking Russian Empire on a war footing had been taken. The chain of events which would lead to World War I had started. On July 19 (August 1, new style) war would be declared.

Кто своею грудью
не отражаетъ
врага
пусть покупаетъ
ВОЕННЫЙ
5½% ЗАЕМЪ
Р. ЗАРРИНЪ

At 3 pm on the afternoon of Sunday July 20 before 5,000 people in the great St George's Hall of the Winter Palace Nicholas II solemnly swore: "I will never make peace so long as one of the enemy is on the soil of the fatherland." It was the same oath sworn by Alexander I when Napoleon invaded Russia in 1812. Before the miraculous icon of the Virgin of Kazan, the most holy in Russia, the throng took up the chant of the national anthem. Here were assembled the grand dukes and duchesses of the Romanov family, the whole Imperial tribe, the nobles of the country whose lineage went back before that of the Romanovs, the great generals and marshals, the officers in their uniforms of scarlet and gold braid, the captains and the courtiers, the ministers, the Patriarch of the Orthodox Church, his metropolitans and bishops, the Czarina, pale and tense at her husband's arm, the Imperial children.

The Czar and Czarina walked slowly through the crowd from the Neva river side of the Palace to the Palace Square and emerged on a balcony. At the sight of Nicholas the hundreds of thousands of plain and ordinary Russians, working men, their wives and children, shopkeepers, businessmen, students and peasants, knelt on the granite paving and the sound of "God Save the Czar" rose from thousands of throats and echoed over the piers of the Neva.

Russian troops smashed easily into Galicia, driving the Austrian forces ahead of them. The Austrian rout falsely lifted Russian hopes that victory might be achieved against the Central Powers.

Nicholas visited the Galician front and congratulated his troops on their successes. Unfortunately, within a few weeks the Russians were compelled to retreat.

FACING PAGE TOP
Russian cavalry in Austrian Galicia where they participated in the capture of the mountain fortress of Pryzyml in late autumn 1914.

FACING PAGE BOTTOM
Despite shortage of guns and munitions the Russians scored occasional successes against their German opponents. Here a German unit in Poland surrenders to advancing Russians.

CHAPTER 5

German Zeppelins drop bombs on Russian targets in World War I.

At first the war went well. The strikes which had crippled St Petersburg in June and early July vanished. Suddenly the factories were turning out more guns, more ammunition, more machines than the railroad flatcars could haul away. The peasants surged in from the villages in such masses that the army could hardly form them all into military units. Millions moved up into the front lines. In the late days of July and early August things seemed to go astonishingly well.

And yet....Rasputin had not been in St Petersburg during the critical days when the issue of war and peace was decided. He was still in Pokrovskoye, his native Siberian village, recuperating from a stab wound inflicted upon him by a jealous lover. He had sent half a dozen telegrams to the Czar and Czarina urging them, begging them, ordering them, not to make war. The Czarina had tried to reason with her husband. But, for once, he acted against her advice, against Rasputin's telegrams. Later, Rasputin would sadly swear that had he been present Russia would not have gone to war.

But his voice was lost in the shouts and cheers. So was that of Count Witte, abroad in southern France at the outbreak of war, who came back grumbling and buttonholing everyone he met with the direst predictions. War would ruin Russia, he said. War would bring down the dynasty. War meant revolution. No one paid heed. The

BELOW AND OPPOSITE
Russian prisoners of war, guarded by Germans in World War 1.

revolutionaries and radicals – by this time many were respectable members of the Duma – were quickly swept up by the police and sent to Siberia. Within a few months every revolutionary organization in Russia had been crushed, the members dispersed, their strength broken for the duration of the war.

Patriotic sentiment carried everything before it. Even radical poets like Mayakovsky and Alexander Blok volunteered. So did Bryusov. For once there was consensus in Russia. The Czar's titanic cousin, Grand Duke Nikolai Nikolaevich, became commander-in-chief. The Russian armies crashed over the frontier into East Prussia, driving the small German units ahead like chaff, or so it seemed from the optimistic reports of General Samsonov. Russian armies pushed into Carpathia, hurling the Austro-Hungarian troops aside. Each evening the victory reports were posted on big bulletins in front of the Petrograd (the Czar had changed the name of his capital because Petersburg was a German word) newspaper offices. In the west the Allies did badly. The German uhlans drove through Belgium. The forts of Liège and Namur fell. German forces swept over France like a river at flood-tide. Alarmed, Paris and London appealed to the Czar. Unless the Russians stepped up their offensive Paris would fall.

The fatal order was given and Samsonov's heavy army trains lumbered forward through the deserted German countryside. Not until they reached the tangle of the Masurian lakes did Hindenburg strike, but when he struck it was a fatal blow.

The battle of Tannenberg has gone down in history as a military classic. The Russians lost 170,000 men. Samsonov shot himself. The threat to East Prussia was liquidated. Worse, the first rumors and suspicions of treachery began to filter through to the Russian public. Samsonov's flank had been exposed by the failure of General Rennekampf to cover him. Rennekampf was a German name. That was enough for the public. (In fact, Rennekampf, like too many generals before and after him, was hoping to gain glory by capturing Koenigsberg and paid no heed to the position of his neighboring general.)

Samsonov's defeat was a shock but fortunately the Russian armies facing Austria advanced so rapidly into Galicia that Austria appealed to Germany for aid – just as France had appealed to Nicholas II. The Germans were compelled to respond. Reserves were held back from the west and the French managed to halt the Germans on the Marne in Joffre's famous battle of the Paris taxicabs. France was saved – but the cost was a wound from which Russia never recovered.

Transportation and communication was endless agony. Mud, bad roads, bad weather and breakdowns of equipment often proved more costly than enemy action.

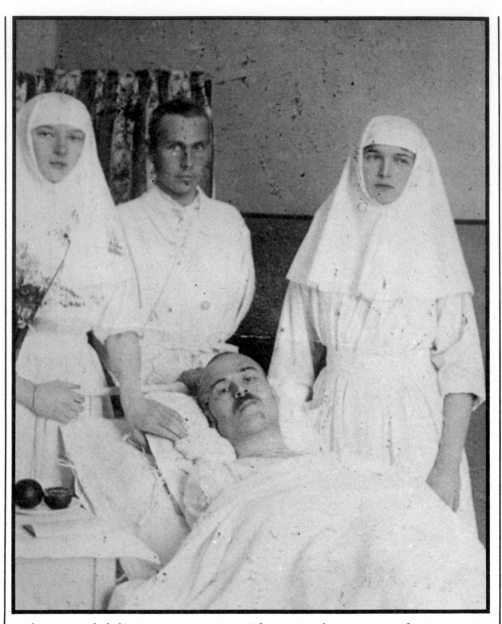

The war settled down to grim attrition. The Russian losses ran at a figure *averaging* 300,000 per month. The supply of rifles was exhausted. Troops were put into the frontlines without arms. They fought with clubs until the death of a comrade freed a rifle. Artillery reserves were exhausted by November 1914. The transportation system fell apart. Despite the impressment of peasants (before the end Russia would mobilize nearly 15,000,000 men) women, children and older men managed to plant and harvest large crops. Since grain could not be exported (the Germans controlled the outlets of the Baltic and their allies, the Turks, the Dardanelles) there was ample food. But it could not be moved to the cities and only with enormous effort was the army kept fed. The cities began to feel the pinch while huge stocks built up in the countryside. In Siberia butter sold for a few kopeks a kilo. In Moscow it could hardly be bought.

At the first signs of economic disintegration, trouble mounted at the front. The Czar and the Czarevich toured the Galician territories seized from Austria. But the triumph proved premature — soon the Russians were forced back, suffering huge losses. Russian factories proved incapable of meeting the front's appetite for guns and ammunition despite energetic efforts by an Industrial-Military Committee composed of those elements in Russian society which the Czar most distrusted — the energetic new entrepreneurs, largely from Moscow.

Matters went from bad to worse. The Czarina pressed her husband to displace Grand Duke Nikolai Nikolaevich and take supreme command. She and Rasputin feared that the Grand Duke was becoming a political rival. Although the Czar's ministers opposed the idea, as did most of the Imperial family, they were unable to sway the Czar.

On August 25 Nicholas telegraphed his wife from "Czar's Stavka", the Czar's General Headquarters that he had taken over. The Czarina's joy was boundless. "Our Friend's [Rasputin's] prayers arise night and day for you to Heaven," she wrote her husband, "and God will hear them.....Your sun is rising. Sleep well my sunshine. Russia's Savior."

The Czar enjoyed Headquarters. Much of the time he had Alexis with him. He thought the military atmosphere was better for the boy than Palace life surrounded by women. He named General Alekseev, a reliable if not brilliant commander, chief-of-staff. By winter the fronts were stabilized. They would change very little during the period of the Czar's command. The war's major action had turned to the west where the demand on German and Allied manpower and material was so heavy that the Russian front sank into lethargy.

Domestic policy fell largely into the hands of the Czarina. The Czar wrote to her: "Think, my wifey, will you not come to the assistance of your hubby now that he is absent?" With those homely words the management of the world's last autocratic empire was placed in the hands of a woman whose principal advisor was the cunning, illiterate, scheming Rasputin. The "Occult Party," as Princess Cantacuzene called it, became supreme.

Mediocrities moved in and out of cabinet offices as if through revolving doors. Scandal piled on scandal. Rasputin made a public exhibition of himself at the Metropol Hotel in Moscow, the police were compelled to intervene and it seemed that his career might come to an end. Instead, the responsible police officers were dismissed. Rumors of German influence in the court grew daily. The Czarina was referred to as "the German" and gossip falsely alleged she was friendly to Russia's enemies. War Minister Sukhomlinov was discharged because of his wife's corrupt dealing in war contracts. The great ballerina, Kshesinskaya, once the Czar's mistress and now the consort of Grand Duke Andrei Vladimirovich, was said to dabble in artillery contracts. Day by day and night by night the atmosphere of Petrograd grew more fetid. Scandals at the gambling halls intensified. Gossip at the Imperial Yacht Club, where the Grand Dukes gathered to drink and talk through lugubrious evenings, grew more heated.

It was apparent even to the Czar and the Czarina that things had gone wrong. But they did not understand what or why. All through 1916 their correspondence dealt with problems of food and supply, the incredible tangle of the railroads. The Czarina hopefully told her husband that Rasputin had a solution. Halt all traffic for a week on the railroads. Devote the lines entirely to moving up food and needed supplies. It would be easy. It took only thirty or forty invalids or old men to load a freight car. Why hadn't they thought of this simple idea before?

The secret police warned the Czar that the mood of the countryside had never been more dangerous; there was open talk of the incompetence of the Government, declarations that "something must be done", growing shortages of food in the cities, rampant inflation. The troops were restive as letters reached the front, telling of the lack of bread, the shortages of boots, of kerosene, salt and candles in the countryside.

The nobility was infected. Talk rose of a coup, of sending the Czarina to a nunnery (an old Russian custom), of plots to do away with Rasputin, to remove the Czar. In the Duma innuendo grew open. Strikes aggravated the situation in the autumn of 1916. Finally Milyukov, the Kadet Party leader, read off in the Duma a list of indictments against the Government, pausing after each count to demand, rhetorically: "Is this stupidity or is this treason?"

The Imperial family launched a final offensive to try to turn Nicholas away from the disastrous policies of the Czarina and Rasputin. The Czar's mother pleaded with him. His powerful cousin, Grand Duke Nikolai Nikolaevich, now commander-in-chief of the Caucasus Front, tried. The liberal Grand Duke Nikolai Mikhailovich tried. So did his brother, George. So did half a dozen other relatives. Nothing changed. The Czarina became more angry. She urged the Czar to hold firm, to show his strength, to "use the knout, the only language the Russians understand". The Czar obeyed his wife.

On November 19, 1916 Vladimir Purishkevich rose in the Duma. Purishkevich was no liberal. He was as reactionary a monarchist as could be found in the Empire. Now he spoke of the "dark forces" which surrounded the Czar. He named names —

Grigory Rasputin, a strannik, or wandering Russian holy man from Pokrovskoye in Siberia, played a major role in the fall of the Romanovs. He won the confidence of Nicholas II and more importantly of Alexandra Feodorovna shortly after the 1905 Revolution. He was a notorious womanizer and it was falsely alleged that the Czarina was among his victims.

Rasputin, Protopopov, Andronikov and the other scoundrels. He called for a tocsin to ring out from the Ivan the Great belltower in the Kremlin and demanded that all who held true to their sovereign make their way to the Czar's Headquarters, throw themselves on their knees and beg leave to tell him of the terrible dangers.

A brilliant young aristocrat, Prince Felix Yusupov, sat in the galleries as Purishkevich spoke. The next day Yusupov called on Purishkevich and told him he was prepared to kill Rasputin. Purishkevich was ready too. Within a day the pair had enlisted the Grand Duke Dmitri Pavlovich, a young cousin and ward of the Czar. The three agreed to act.

Plots to kill Rasputin had become a commonplace of Petrograd gossip. Now a real plan was swiftly elaborated by men determined to carry it out. It was a simple plan. Yusupov had made Rasputin's acquaintance, he would lure him to his Palace. There the conspirators would kill Rasputin, take his body and hurl it into the Neva river.

On the evening of December 16 Rasputin accompanied young Yusupov to the Palace where Yusupov had invited him to meet his attractive wife, who was, in fact, with her parents in the Crimea. The plotters poisoned some wine and cakes with cyanide (Rasputin had a sweet tooth and drank nothing but sweet wine) and armed themselves with revolvers.

Once Rasputin arrived nothing went well. At first Yusupov, for some reason, didn't offer Rasputin the poisoned cake and wine. Later when Rasputin did partake they seemed to have no effect. Yusupov lost his nerve and ran off to consult his fellow conspirators. Finally Rasputin became befuddled, whether by the wine or the poison no one was ever to know. Yusupov drew a revolver and shot him. The conspirators danced with joy about Rasputin's body which lay on a white bearskin rug. As they set about arranging to dispose of the corpse Rasputin suddenly opened his eyes and clutched at Yusupov who screamed in horror and ran off. Purishkevich, more level-headed, came to the rescue. As Rasputin struggled to escape through the Palace garden, Purishkevich shot at him four times. One or two of the bullets took effect and the body was lugged back inside the Palace with the help of some passing soldiers.

The conspirators managed to load the body into a car and dump it from a bridge into the icy waters of the Malaya Nevka, a tributary of the Neva. Police came around to investigate but were not able to determine what had happened.

The next day the conspirators began to tell people what they had done but even so it took the police forty-eight hours to unravel the murder and recover Rasputin's body.

The Czar hurried back from headquarters to comfort his heartbroken wife. A private mass was said over Rasputin's body and it was buried in the Imperial grounds at Tsarskoye Selo. The participants were banished from Petrograd – Purishkevich to the front, the Grand Duke Dmitri to Persia and Yusupov to his family estates. Now, many in Petrograd felt, the course of the Government would change, responsible ministers would be brought in, the Duma would be given a hand in running affairs, and the war would be prosecuted with vigor.

Nothing of the kind happened. The Czar and Czarina, more alone, more cut off than ever, did not change course. Police reported the level of unrest steadily rising. Never had it been so palpable. Only one thing was lacking, an event to trigger the people into action. It might come at any moment. When it did it would not be an organized coup. There were no revolutionaries to start anything. All were in exile, in prison or abroad. It would be a people's uprising, the most dangerous of all Russian events. Reports and rumors came to the surface daily. The military, it was said, had decided to act. (They had, in fact, talked of acting but could not agree on what action to take.) The Grand Dukes again spoke of taking a hand (but could not decide what hand they wanted to take). The situation drifted. On February 10, 1917, Rodzyanko, the powerful Centrist Duma leader, had tea with the Czar. The Czar was irritable and hostile. Nonetheless, Rodzyanko spoke his mind. If a responsible government was not formed "the result of this will be a revolution and anarchy which no one will be able to control".

The Czar made no reply. He icily showed Rodzyanko to the door. It was the last time the two were to meet. On February 22 the Czar left Petrograd for his military headquarters at Mogilev. His ministers assured him all was quiet in the capital. There was no reason for him to worry.

Food was short and there were lines for everything. A **92** *milk queue in Moscow.*

Desertions from the front line were numbered in the hundreds of thousands. Sometimes troops fought each other. Here a soldier attacks two deserters with his rifle butt. Such scenes were not common. Most of the troops simply streamed away from the lines, clogging railroads and transport beyond imagination.

CHAPTER 6

Russia's artists quickly enlisted in the cause of the Bolshevik regime. This poster depicts Lenin cleaning up the world — sweeping away capitalists, kings and generals.

Тов. Ленин ОЧИЩАЕТ землю от нечисти.

With the outbreak of war on August 1, 1914 the Austrian authorities arrested Lenin at Poronin and confined him to this prison cell in Novy Targ on suspicion of espionage. He was released a few days later and permitted to go to Switzerland on the affirmation of the Austrian Socialist Adler that Lenin was a more convinced opponent of the Czarist Government than was the Austrian Government. Lenin was confined in this cell in Novy Targ until August 6, 1914.

FACING PAGE
Lenin and the writer Maxim Gorky in Petrograd for the Second Congress of the Communist International. Lenin and Gorky had been very close before the Revolution but Gorky broke with Lenin over the Bolshevik coup. After Lenin was seriously wounded in an assassination attempt in August 1918, there was a partial reconciliation.

enin never had a worse winter than that of 1917. He was arrested in Austrian Galicia at the outbreak of war in 1914 and for a few days he had been frightened for his life but the Austrian Socialist leader, Victor Adler (Adler and Lenin were bitter political enemies), intervened and got Lenin released on condition that he went to Switzerland. Adler swore Lenin was an even more staunch foe of the Russian government than the Austrians.

The war years had been grim. Lenin was almost without connections to Russia. Weeks went by with no reports from Petrograd. His Bolshevik organization had been smashed by the Czar's police. He kept himself occupied with the Social Democratic movement in Europe — in France, in Scandinavia and, particularly, in Switzerland. He even explored the revolutionary cause in the United States. He argued with his fellow Russian exiles and he quarrelled violently with the various sects of Socialists and Social Democrats. He wrote furious articles but could seldom persuade anyone to publish them and he had so little money that his own Party newspaper, a four-page leaflet, came out only occasionally and in editions of 200 or 300 copies which he tried to smuggle into Russia.

Lenin's nerves, never sturdy, became more and more strained. He was a man of strong passions and had been since the days when he was growing up in a middle-class Russian family in the provincial Volga city of Simbirsk (now Ulyanovsk). His father had been awarded a minor rank in the nobility for faithful work in the schools, and his mother was the daughter of a well-to-do surgeon and landowner, a woman of high moral principles who dedicated herself to her husband and family of three boys and two girls. Lenin had been reared in conventional manner and was headed for a brilliant career as an advocate or lawyer. But his father died suddenly and within a year his older brother, Alexander, an even better student than Lenin at St Petersburg University, fell in with a small group of students who decided almost by whim to try to assassinate Czar Alexander III, father of Nicholas II.

Alexander joined in the attempt which could hardly have been worse bungled. The bombs which Alexander made were not thrown and police inspection disclosed they would never have exploded had they been thrown. But the young plotters were arrested and Alexander and four others were hanged.

Alexander's death left an indelible impression on Lenin. He got his law degree but the only profession he ever practiced was that of revolutionary. He turned against his brother's dedication to terrorism — a heritage of the People's Will movement. Lenin became, instead, a believer in Karl Marx' economic determinism. Lenin elaborated his own theory of Revolution which he concluded could only be brought about by a dedicated band of professional conspirators directed from abroad. The leader of the group, naturally, must be himself.

Lenin was violently contentious. He fought with his fellow revolutionaries, denouncing anyone who did not fully agree with him. Again and again he made it plain that rather than compromise his views he was prepared to split his group even if he became the sole surviving member.

Lenin was respected, feared but not loved by his fellow radicals. The year 1917 found him almost isolated. His principal supporters were members of his own family — his two sisters, his brother and a brother-in-law in Russia and his faithful wife, Nadezhda Krupskaya, who carried on much of the burden of organization and correspondence. A handful of other dedicated sympathizers stood by Lenin, among them a beautiful Russianized Frenchwoman, Inessa Armand, then living in Switzerland with whom Lenin had a long, intense and intimate relationship.

Later on Bolshevik historians would falsify the record, trying to make it seem that Lenin was the mainspring and the prophet of the Revolution. But the reality as recorded by Lenin himself was quite the opposite. He and Krupskaya lived those pre-revolutionary years alone and in penury in Switzerland. They had few contacts with Russia. Lenin was so short of funds he was willing to write almost any article for money and had abandoned his fierce insistence that his articles not be cut or edited.

He recorded his despair of revolution in a frank and doleful lecture which he read to some young Swiss on the twelfth anniversary of the 1905 uprising, January 9, 1917. Most of his talk dealt with Europe. He doubted that those like himself of the older

Lenin's nickname from the 1890's was "Starik" – old man. He became prematurely bald and his high forehead and naked pate made the appellation natural. He often used it as a conspiratorial signature.

When Lenin was compelled to flee Petrograd in July 1917 for fear of arrest by Kerensky he donned a wig and wore working men's clothes while being smuggled on a railroad locomotive across the border to Finland.

In Paris, sometime in 1910, Lenin met Inessa Armand, a vibrant woman who became the passion of his life. Inessa took a house next door to that of Lenin and Krupskaya in Paris and the lives of the three were joined closely until their return to Russia in April 1917. Krupskaya is said to have offered to divorce Lenin, but he refused.

Moscow was a run-down city in the early days of the Revolution. Here Lenin and his younger sister Maria make their way to the Fifth All Russian Congress of Soviets in 1918.

Signature du Titulaire:

Léon Trotsky

generation would live to see the flame of revolution rise again in Russia.

It was for Lenin a long, cold, tedious winter. He wrote plaintively to his beloved Inessa on February 28, worrying that he might have offended her. His letter sounded tired and forlorn. He said he had no news whatever from Russia, not even a letter. He did not know that in Petrograd the February "events" – the February Revolution as it came to be known – had already been underway for five days.

If the case of Lenin seems dramatic it is only because history (and propaganda) have so intimately associated his name with the Russian Revolution. The other revolutionaries like Lenin had no connection with, nor foreknowledge of, the coming February uprising. Trotsky, for example, was in the Bronx. He had wound up there with his family a few months before, having been deported, on the complaint of the Russian Embassy, from France where he was editing a radical Russian newspaper. Trotsky had followed his own individualistic course since 1905. His views and those of

СТОРОЖ РЕВО

Trotsky speaks from the top of an armored car called "On Guard of the Revolution".

Lenin were not far apart but like many radicals they put differences ahead of agreements and indulged in violent polemics. Trotsky, son of a well-to-do Jewish manufacturer in south Russia, was hard at work on a radical Russian newspaper published on New York's lower East Side. One of his colleagues was Nikolai Bukharin who would soon play a brilliant role in the Bolshevik Party (until shot by Stalin in the 1930's purges). Lenin, as usual, was outraged by Trotsky. He believed he had taken over the New York paper. "What a swine this Trotsky is!" he wrote to Alexandra Kollontai, one of his supporters who was also in America.

Plekhanov, the founder of Russia's Marxist movement and once Lenin's idol, was living in embittered exile in Paris far out of the mainstream of Russian events. Viktor Chernov, the brilliant leader of the Socialist Revolutionary Party whose campaign of assassination and terror had been the dread of the Czarist Okhrana and gained the Socialist Revolutionaries wider support than any other leftist party in Russia, was

Lenin enjoyed vacationing in the mountains and when he transferred headquarters of the Bolshevik operations from Paris to Cracow in 1911 he liked to spend the summers in the Galician mountains.

Lenin played politics as he played chess. He was so fond of chess that he compelled himself to put the game aside, for it interfered with his concentration on Revolution. Here he plays in Capri in 1908 as Maxim Gorky looks on.

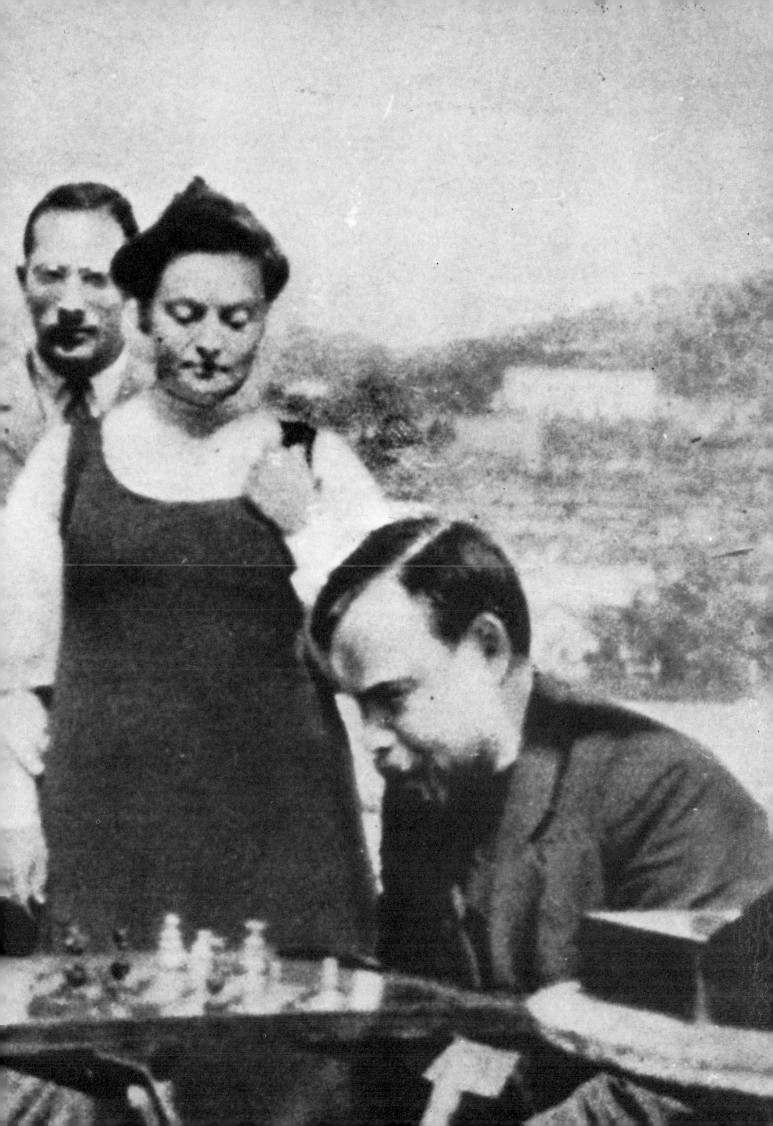

These troops hold a banner declaring "God is With Us".

also in Paris, as cut off from his homeland as Lenin. His party organization was in ruins. His associate Natanson was in Switzerland, as were Martov and Axelrod, the Menshevik leaders. Dozens of Revolutionaries rusticated in distant Siberian exile: Dan and Tsereteli among the Mensheviks, Catherine Breshko-Breshkovsky, the famous SR leader, together with her colleague, Abram Gotz.

What of Lenin's Bolsheviks? Almost all the middle echelon was in Siberia. Stalin, a young but trusted associate of Lenin's from the Caucasus, had been there since 1912. Kamenev, Muranov and Sverdlov and many others had been exiled in the autumn of 1914. They had no communication with Lenin in Switzerland and virtually none with Moscow and Petrograd. No longer was it possible to escape from exile simply by hiring a sleigh or walking to the nearest railroad.

For practical purposes, as the Czar's police accurately reported, the organized revolutionary movements were out of business. Out of business, dispirited, disheartened. There was not one individual of those named above who after the February events could look back to his correspondence, his diary or his pamphlets and say – there, on such-and-such a day, I predicted it would happen.

If the Czar, the Czarina and the corrupt and stupid inner circle which surrounded them did not believe that Russia was about to explode it could be said that their lack of vision was fully shared by Lenin and his revolutionary colleagues and competitors. If Lenin and his fellow revolutionaries were practising the "science of Revolution" as proclaimed by Marx, all that can be said is that as a science it was no more exact than the table-tipping to which the Czarina and her friends were addicted.

Sir George Buchanan, the British Ambassador to Petrograd, was a resolute and courageous man. He had a foreboding that events in Russia were moving toward catastrophe and, after obtaining permission from the Foreign Office to speak on his own (and at the risk of being declared *persona non grata*), sought an audience with Nicholas II and frankly told him that unless he placed a strong man at the head of the Government and began to work with the Duma revolution and disaster was likely.

The Czar listened without apparent anger and departed for General Headquarters at Mogilev. Buchanan, feeling he had done all he could, went off to Finland for a short holiday. He heard no rumors there disturbing enough to interrupt his holiday. In fact, had not the February "events" intervened the Czar almost certainly would have demanded that London recall Buchanan. One of the Czarina's last letters to her husband reminded him to write his cousin King George V "about Buchanan".

Madame Kshesinskaya, the ballerina and former mistress of Nicholas II, had been concerned about possible disturbances in Petrograd and she, too, went off to Finland for a holiday with her son Vova and the dancer P. N. Vladimirov. Everything seemed so quiet, however, that she came back to Petrograd and gave a dinner party for twenty-four on Wednesday, February 22. She used her Limoges service, gilt knives and forks copied from sets belonging to Catherine II on exhibition at the Hermitage, and put on display many valuable objects of art including a priceless collection of artificial flowers made of precious stones and a small gold fir tree whose branches shimmered with small diamonds.

The French Ambassador, Maurice Paléologue, was a bit more concerned. Petrograd was short of bread and wood, and heavy snow and extreme cold was delaying the trains bringing supplies into the Russian capital. He knew that queues were growing before the bread shops.

Thursday February 23 was International Women's Day. It was no big event in Petrograd but it brought some women factory workers into the streets where they were joined by workers of the Putilov steel plant who had gone on strike.

Madame Kshesinskaya was later to remember that her son, Vova, ran into her great house just beyond the Troitsky bridge over the Neva and said he had seen a huge throng on Bolshaya Dvoryanskaya Street. Count de Robien, a young attaché at the French Embassy, was impressed by the crowds on Nevsky Prospekt and noticed that the streetcars on the Sadovaya had been halted. But no one seemed very excited.

An officer of a Guards regiment wearing a baby bow red armband.

Ambassador Paléologue heard people shouting for bread. The lines for bread were noticably longer and many bakeries ran out of supplies. This didn't keep the Ambassador from giving a great dinner party at the Embassy with the Prince and Princess Gorchakov, Countess Kleinmichel, Count Tolstoy, the director of the Hermitage Collections, the Vicomtesse du Halgouet, the Princess Dolgoruky, the Marquis of Villasinda and the artist Alexander Benois and his wife among the guests. There was some talk at the dinner party about the food situation, but a good deal more about the ballerinas of the Mariinsky theater. The diners argued the question of which among the big three, Pavlova, Kshesinskaya and Karsavina, was the most brilliant.

The weather was unusually mild and sunny and on Friday 24, the great boulevards, the Nevsky in particular, were thronged from side to side. Everyone in the city seemed to be turning out. Most of the factories were closing down. Workers poured into the center, many of them crossing over the frozen Neva. Mounted Cossack troops had been ordered out on patrol but there was little violence. The crowds were cheerful and joked with the troops. Most of the mounted soldiers were unusually polite as they rode through the crowds. Some bakeries were stormed, windows broken and stocks looted, particularly in the Vyborg workers quarter and some observers were beginning to worry that the trouble might be serious. But Ambassador Paléologue was assured that everything would be all right if Interior Minister Protopopov, a protégé of Rasputin, would attend to business. Protopopov was said to be spending much of his time in spirit seances, conferring with Rasputin's ghost. Several diplomats were received that afternoon by the Czarina at the Tsarskoye Selo palace. They reported Alexandra calm but she told them that there was danger "when the people are hungry". However, she felt certain that the army was loyal and could be relied upon.

A naval officer in pseudo-proletarian garb or, alternatively, a radical agitator in pseudo-naval garb.

The Czar spent his time quietly at Mogilev Headquarters. He had received only casual reports about the situation in Petrograd, nothing alarming. He missed his son, Alexis, who usually accompanied him and he was worried because all of the children as well as Madame Vyrubova were down with the measles. He wrote his wife about taking the family to the Crimea and the sunshine soon after Easter. The rooms at Tsarskoye Selo would have to be disinfected. They could, of course, move temporarily to the grandiose Peterhof Palace but neither he nor his wife cared for it. "Where can we live then?" he asked his wife. "We shall think this out in peace on my return home which I hope will be soon!" He said that his brain was at rest. "I shall not be away long — direct things as best I can here," he wrote, "and then my duty will be fulfilled."

That Friday for the first time observers in Petrograd heard occasional cries of Down with the War! Down with the Monarchy!

CHAPTER 17

Revolution brought down the great statue of Czar Alexander III which had been erected in the Cathedral court of the Moscow Kremlin. Workmen ascended the metal figure, broke it to bits and toppled it to the ground.

The Litovsky prison in flames. The postcard is enscribed: "Hurrah! Greetings to Freedom!"

It was on Saturday February 25 that the conviction began to spread that Petrograd was in the grip of something more than the usual strikes and protests. The authorities had sent substantially more troops into the streets and proclamations appeared on the walls warning that if strikers did not return to work they would be conscripted into the army. Despite the warning the work stoppage was total. Not a cab, not a doorman, not a bank clerk was on duty. Streetcars halted and everyone poured into the streets, possibly a majority of the city's 2,500,000 population.

Despite the massive demonstrations the troops were under orders not to fire — the ministers were fearful that photographs of shooting and bodies on the pavement would produce a negative reaction from the western Allies and make the raising of huge war-time foreign loans difficult. Speakers appeared in the public squares and began to harangue the crowds but there was no pattern of agitation. Some of the speakers were students, some workers, some ordinary middle-class citizens.

The soldiers seemed as interested in what was being said as the crowds. When Cossack troopers with sabres and tall fur hats appeared people shouted: "Hurrah!" The Cossacks touched their caps and rode quietly through the crowd taking care that their horses did not injure anyone. This was a new development. For two generations the hostility between Cossacks and street crowds in Russia had been legendary. Now something had changed and those who noticed it felt in the presence of something extraordinary. What it might mean no one yet knew but some city officials and military officers felt a sudden chill. If there was trouble what would be the role of the Czar's crack regiments? Would they stand — as always in the past — with the Imperial eagle? Or with the people?

All day long General Khabalov, the Petrograd commandant, watched the situation with growing concern. In late afternoon Constable Krylov, leader of a detachment of mounted police, was shot and killed in Znamenskaya Square by a member of a Cossack detachment. Krylov was the first fatality of the "February events". The fact that he was a policeman and had been killed by a soldier gave his death special significance. A bit later there was gunfire outside the City Duma and three persons were killed and nine wounded. A number of police were injured.

It was obvious that the news must be reported to the Czar. General Khabalov sent a not very alarming report to Mogilev and Interior Minister Protopopov emphasized that the military was taking firm measures and that there was no trouble in Moscow. The Czar got two telegrams from his wife. The first said that the city was "still quiet". The second said things were not yet normal.

The Czar remained more concerned about the outbreak of measles among his children than the disorders in his capital. However, he decided that a show of force was in order. He telegraphed Khabalov ordering him to bring the disturbances to an end on Sunday. The disorders were not, he said, "permissible in a time of difficult war with Germany and Austria".

Khabalov was in a quandary. He was not sure he could carry out the Czar's instructions. However, he called in his lieutenants and told them that tomorrow the troops were to give the crowds three warnings. If they did not disperse the order was to fire with live ammunition.

The political leaders were no more confident than the military. A group of liberal and radical figures met informally at the apartment of the writer, Maxim Gorky. They didn't have much idea of what was going on. Two or three junior Bolsheviks came in. Their principal interests seemed to be to get out leaflets and organize workers. Alexander Kerensky, a left liberal Duma member, ran around in great excitement. He said the Duma had no idea of what to do in the crisis. There was an angry meeting at the City Duma where violent protests were made about the shooting of demonstrators by the troops. The secret police carried out a series of raids, arresting suspected revolutionaries, among them Lenin's sister, Anna. The President of the Duma, Rodzyanko, tried to persuade Premier Golitsyn to resign. Golitsyn replied by showing Rodzyanko a blank form the Czar had given him. It already bore the Czar's signature and ordered the Duma prorogued.

The Council of Ministers argued about what they ought to do until 4 am Sunday

morning, then adjourned and made their way home without having done anything. Troops patrolled the streets and stood guard at the bridges. The city was dark and quiet.

The Council of Ministers again met in a long, agonized session. For the first time the reliability of the Petrograd garrison was questioned and there was talk of getting in new troops and of relieving Khabalov of his command. Finally it was decided to announce a state of siege and prorogue the Duma, using one of the Czar's blank forms. The Duma members conducted equally indecisive discussions. Kerensky grew more and more excited. Several Bolshevik underlings insisted that there was not, and would not be, a revolution. The thing to do was to prepare for a long period of underground activity. Many thought the Government was deliberately provoking the crowds in order to crush them and install a military dictatorship.

The Czar was irritated by the telegram he had received from Rodzyanko. "Once again that fat Rodzyanko has written me some kind of rubbish," he exclaimed. He wrote to his wife that he had suffered sharp chest pains while attending church services but now felt better. He expressed hope that Khabalov would quickly bring the disorders to an end.

But later in the evening, after receiving more reports of what was happening in Petrograd, he decided to return to his capital on Tuesday. He played dominoes until it was time to go to his bed.

Few who lived through Monday February 27 in Petrograd ever forgot a detail of the day. Members of the Duma gathered early at the Tauride Palace. No one had issued a call for them to assemble. They simply gravitated there. Before noon the great palace was filled with men trying to understand the meaning of what was in progress, trying to understand what their role should be. The Duma was not exactly a revolutionary stronghold. The members were parliamentarians, many of them Conservatives and supporters of the monarchy. The last thing which they wanted was to become the center of a revolution which would bring down the 300-year rule of the Romanovs.

Yet it was quickly clear to men like Rodzyanko that the Duma had become the eye of the hurricane. As, one by one, the Czar's crack regiments moved into the streets of Petrograd and joined the crowds in demolishing the symbols of Czarist power the Duma emerged as the only instrument of authority.

Soon word spread through Tauride Palace that troops and workers were headed there. What was the Duma to do? It was a tricky question. The Duma had been prorogued by the Czar. Technically, at least, it had no legal function. Finally, it was agreed to form a "Provisional Committee" of all parties except those of the right. The purpose of the Committee was to restore order and establish contact with public organizations and institutions; in a word, to fill the power vacuum which was being created by the dissolution of the Czarist government.

Hardly had the new Committee been formed than those within the Tauride Palace heard a distant murmur which grew louder until it swelled into a noise like rolling thunder. This was the sound of tramping feet, of shouting voices. It was the sound of the people of Petrograd, thousands upon thousands of them, marching to the Tauride Palace, surrounding it, enveloping it, engulfing it.

The crowd filled the courtyards, it surged into the palace, it thronged the corridors and flowed into the halls and chambers. No Duma member had ever seen anything like it. Nor had anyone in Petrograd. There *had* never been anything like it.

Some members were in panic. They thought they would be lynched. But not Kerensky. He rushed to greet the soldiers and workers, to join and unify their aspirations and emotions with those of the Duma. Quickly other Duma leaders took up this posture, welcoming the people, haranguing them in the name of the Revolution. Without anyone quite noticing, the "February events" became on that Monday afternoon the "February Revolution," a revolution in which not a single revolutionary had yet played any role. It had been made by ordinary citizens, particularly by angry women, housewives sick and tired of standing in freezing queues before empty shops, and by sympathetic soldiers who felt their role was with the people rather than with the distant Czar and his bureaucrats. To only a few of those in the Tauride Palace that afternoon was the meaning of this complex yet simple transition clear and even later confusion persisted over what had happened, how it had happened and why it had happened.

In the course of attacks on the prisons some radicals and revolutionaries were released, most of them from the lower echelons, and these men and women began to drift toward the Tauride Palace. For several days the factories had been naming members to a Soviet or Council such as had been set up in 1905 and a meeting of these delegates, together with representatives of the troops, was called for the evening of the 27th at 7 pm at the Tauride. The handful of Lenin's Bolsheviks in Petrograd had no part in this, as they would in time acknowledge. They did not think the Soviet was important. Later their absence could be seen as of great historical importance — for later on the Bolsheviks insisted that they had led the Revolution in which, in fact, they had no role whatsoever.

The morning of Sunday February 26, was spring-like. The ice was melting from the roofs and gutters of the great old Petrograd palaces. The bells of the churches sounded. The sun glinted off their gilded onion domes. The chant of the Orthodox mass resounded

Armed detachments of Bolshevik Red Guards, factory workers, students, sailors of the Baltic fleet and some Bolshevik sympathizers among the military garrison range the streets of Petrograd.

ПОМНИ ГОЛОДАЮЩИХ!

in the ears of the faithful. The streets were quiet and orderly. The Czarina wrote her husband that she was certain everything would work out all right.

"The sun shines so clearly and I felt such peace and quiet at His [Rasputin's] dear grave," she wrote. "He died in order to save us."

General Khabalov, greatly reassured, telegraphed the Czar: "The City is quiet." But Rodzyanko felt it was a false dawn. The trouble, as he saw it, was already critical and worse lay ahead. He went to Defense Minister Belyaev and General Khabalov to protest the soldiers firing on the people. Why shouldn't they use fire hoses against the crowds? And what was being done to bring in more food supplies?

Rodzyanko could get no satisfactory answers and, his concern rising, sent a telegram warning the Czar that there was anarchy in Petrograd and that a new government must be formed without delay or the consequences might be irrevocable.

Even as Rodzyanko was drafting his telegram firing broke out on the Nevsky Prospekt. Some forty people were killed and many more wounded at Znamenskaya Square. There were less serious outbursts at other places. For the first time some members of the crowd had armed themselves with revolvers and hand grenades.

Most serious of all, a detachment of the crack Pavlovsky regiment, arms in hand, issued from its barracks and exchanged fire with a unit of the mounted police. Colonel Eksten, commander of the Pavlovskys, was killed. This was mutiny, no less, in one of the most honored of the Czar's regiments. True, the Guards regiments like the

Pavlovsky were represented in Petrograd by reserve detachments. True, the reserve detachments were diluted with conscripts many of whom were impressed factory workers. True, the officers were not always of the rank and purity of the nobility. Nonetheless, the revolt of the Pavlovskys was a turning point. No longer could one speak of the February "events" as casual street disorders. Whether the Pavlovskys knew it or not (and the evidence is clear that they were swept up by anger and acted heedless of consequences and with no understanding of the significance of their action) they had committed a genuinely revolutionary act.

Late February 1917. The crisis grows. The Duma meets for the last time under the portrait of Nicholas II by Repin. In a day or two soldiers with their bayonets will rip it out of its frame and the Czar will be overthrown.

CHAPTER 8

Red Guards prepare for combat in the Crimea in 1918.

116

The Government rapidly disintegrated. The Council of Ministers assembled at the Mariinsky Palace and tried to find troops to restore order. Hardly any were available. A few thousand were finally gathered in the square before the Winter Palace. A state of siege was proclaimed, but the Government had no way of announcing this to the people nor any troops to enforce it. The hated Interior Minister Protopopov was sent packing. He announced there was nothing left to do but commit suicide. Instead, he went into hiding in a tailor's shop and turned himself over to the Duma the next day.

Frantic messages were sent to Mogilev and, finally, some sense of crisis began to come through to the Czar. He ordered that crack troops be withdrawn from the fronts and dispatched to Petrograd and sent a general named Ivanov with a small force to reconnoitre the situation and, if feasible, take over the capital under dictatorial powers. He himself proposed to leave shortly after midnight and return to Tsarskoye Selo.

As the evening wore on the situation in Petrograd grew more desperate. The Ministers at the Mariinsky Palace began to disperse. Rebellious troops closed in. For a while the small detachment of loyal forces huddled in the Winter Palace then, after midnight, the dispirited band of 1,500 troops moved over to the spire-topped Admiralty, there to stay, gradually trickling away, until they were ordered out the next day at noon by the Naval Minister.

The Czarina viewed developments with alarm. She telegraphed her husband three times during the day, each time warning that the situation was becoming critical. She may also have spoken with him by direct telephone – an extremely rare event, for neither the Czar nor the Czarina liked to use the telephone. It was regarded by them as a kind of vulgarity, almost a form of *lèse majesté*. At one point she suggested that she and the children (not yet recovered from the measles) meet the Czar en route to Tsarskoye Selo. But the Czar would have none of this. Troops were on the way. He was returning. Everything would be put right. It could not have entered his mind that even before he left Mogilev he had, in fact, lost his Empire.

The truth was that the Czar's government had dissolved. There was at this moment in Russia, as Milyukov, the leader of the centrist Kadet party was to observe later: "No Czar, no Duma, no Council of Ministers."

This became dramatically apparent that evening at the Tauride Palace. There in the Catherine Hall the Soviet assembled under the chairmanship of Chkheidze, a Menshevik leader and sworn opponent of Lenin. In this hall, jammed with working men and women and soldiers in long greatcoats, many still carrying their rifles, their boots muddy, regiment after regiment declared its allegiance to the cause of the people. As each name of a great regiment was called out the hall rang with cheers. It was the roll call of the end of an era. No one had yet proclaimed it but 300 years of Romanov regime had ended. It was vanishing before the eyes of those present in the Tauride Palace. The tattered band of soldiers which crowded into the hall to give their testimonials were the masters of the Empire – but they did not know this. Nor did the nervous parliamentarians. At any moment, they feared, the Czar's troops might appear and drive all before them. At intervals the Menshevik leader Chkheidze was seized with terror. All was lost – so he thought. If the Czar didn't regain power the soldiers would drive the civilians out and put a Napoleon in their place. The night wore on. Again and again Rodzyanko told himself: "I am not a revolutionary." But finally he gave in. The Duma Provisional Committee agreed to take power into its hands lest it fall into the possession of others.

On Tuesday morning Petrograd awakened to find proclamations on the walls declaring that the Duma Committee had found it necessary to take upon itself the task of re-establishing government and social order.

The Czar's train left Headquarters for Tsarskoye Selo characteristically behind time. It did not chuff away until 5 am on Tuesday morning and it spent the day moving slowly across the pleasant snowbound Russian countryside. At the last minute the Czar's Chief of Staff, General Alekseev, tried to persuade Nicholas not to go. Alekseev was not the only one who thought the journey ill-omened. But the Czar's mind was made up. He shrugged off the protests.

It was a pleasant day. The weather was marvellous. There was no news from

Petrograd. The Czar strolled in the sunshine when the train halted for coal and water and sent the Czarina a telegram, hoping she was not too disturbed, he would be back soon. Many troops were coming to the capital from the front. The spirits of the Czar's entourage rose. It was hard to believe that anything very serious was taking place. Certainly nothing like a revolution. As usual, it began to be believed, the bureaucrats in Petrograd had become hysterical over trifles.

The Czar had a pleasant dinner and at about 9 pm the train halted at Likhoslavl. The Czar got a telegram from his wife. She was relieved that he was well and that he would be arriving in the morning. But there was other news. All bad. For the first time the Czar heard of the Duma Provisional Committee taking power. He heard that a man named Bublikov was now in charge of the railroads – his railroads – that the Winter Palace had been plundered and the Mayor of Petrograd shot. The rumors about the Winter Palace and the Mayor were not true. But the Czar had no way of knowing that. There was also a report that the Imperial train would be intercepted by the revolutionaries and would not be permitted to go on to Tsarskoye Selo.

After an hysterical discussion the train resumed its progress and about 2.30 am on Wednesday March 1, arrived at Malaya Vishera a little more than 100 miles southeast of Petrograd. A railwayman said further progress was impossible; the rebels had seized the next station, Lyuban. It was decided to head for Northern Front Headquarters at Pskov and consult there with General Ruzsky about further steps.

All day long on Wednesday, March 1, the mood on the Czar's train rose again. There were long discussions. The Czar decided at long last to accept a constitutional monarchy and he was expecting to meet at Pskov with Rodzyanko, the President of the Duma, and announce his decision. This would mean that "fat old Rodzyanko" whom the Czar so much disliked would become Prime Minister. Even to that, the Czar was reconciled.

But events in Petrograd now moved with a rapidity which the Czar could not sense. At Pskov it became clear that what the Czar proposed was too little and too late. Rodzyanko decided not to come to Pskov after all. A new solution was being mooted: that Nicholas should abdicate in favor of his son Alexis, and a regent, presumably the Grand Duke Michael.

Thursday March 2 was the fateful day. Ruzsky told the Czar of Rodzyanko's conclusion – that abdication was in order. Then he gave the Czar the replies to a round-robin telegram he had sent to the top-ranking generals. Their unanimous view was that the Czar must go. Word arrived that two emissaries from the Duma were en route, Deputies Shulgin and Guchkov, both monarchists. They were coming to request the Czar's abdication. By now the Czar had decided: "I will give up the throne."

That evening, in the sumptuous private railroad car which served as his reception room, the Czar signed the formal act of abdication in favor of his brother, the Grand Duke Michael, relinquishing the throne on behalf of himself and his son, Alexis. The Czar's action on behalf of his son was, strictly speaking, illegal but he took the step after being told by his physician that Alexis' illness was incurable.

There was no ceremony about the abdication, just a businesslike meeting in the railroad car. Then the Czar left for a final farewell to his military staff at Mogilev.

On March 23, 1917 a million
people marched through the
streets of Petrograd to pay
tribute to the 184 persons
who died in the Revolution.
They were buried in the
Champs de Mars to the
rolling thunder of 184
cannon, flaming torches
lighting the great open space.
When the guns had stilled
there was total silence.

CHAPTER 9

The young Justice Minister in the Provisional Government, Alexander F. Kerensky, quickly emerged as its most dynamic member. He ranged the front lines, often persuading soldiers to stay in the trenches and fight through the force of his oratory.

The Provisional Government got off to a shaky start. It was a democratic bourgeois government, headed by Prince Lvov, well-meaning, public-spirited but hardly a strong man. The conservative Guchkov became Minister of Defense but did not last long. The experienced Milyukov took the portfolio of Foreign Affairs. He was a strong supporter of the Allies and the best-known and ablest democratic spokesman in Russian politics. But his determination to stand by the Czarist agreements with France and Britain, his pro-war policy, his antipathy for revolutionary rhetoric and his unwillingness or inability to compromise doomed him to early resignation.

From the beginning there was intense competition between the Provisional Government, which was the creation of the Provisional Committee of the Duma, and the ad hoc Soviet, the true creature of the Revolution, directly representing the workers and the soldiers. The Soviet was the milieu of the more radical movements and there was constant friction between the Government and the Soviet. Neither had the power or authority to suppress the other. Neither was willing to give the other a free hand.

There was one man who moved easily, effectively and dramatically in this environment. This was the tall, slim, handsome, eloquent 36-year-old lawyer, Alexander Kerensky, Minister of Justice in the Provisional Government and simultaneously a member of the Executive Committee of the Soviet. He belonged to a small party closely allied to the Socialist Revolutionaries, possessed boundless energy and an instinctive feeling for crowds and the dramatic moment.

Kerensky and Lenin came from the same Volga city, Simbirsk, and from an almost identical background. Kerensky's father was the principal of the school attended by Lenin, his sisters and their martyred older brother, Alexander. Lenin's father, Ilya, was school inspector for the whole middle Volga district. The elder Ulyanov and the elder Kerensky were close friends.

Because of his unusual character, his boldness and his effectiveness in speaking to the revolutionary crowds, Kerensky swiftly became the outstanding figure in turbulent Petrograd.

He swept from meeting to meeting, now addressing factory workers, now talking to the throngs of soldiers crowding the trains and leaving the front in increasing numbers. Now he paused a moment to startle his Provisional Government colleagues with some melodramatic pose; a bit later he would by force of dramatic oratory carry the day in the contentious Soviet.

No one swam in the rushing waters of the early Revolution as did Kerensky. Not even Lenin.

Lenin at his desk reading Pravda.

Lenin did not dawdle in Switzerland once he became convinced that the news of the uprising in Petrograd was genuine. True, his first reaction was one of scepticism. He had not anticipated anything like this. He hedged his comments, in writing to his dear friend Inessa Armand, with remarks like "if it is true", "if the reports are accurate". Even after the Czar's abdication he still thought it was a trick pulled off by the British and French with the aid of the big Russian capitalists. He had no sense of the popular nature of the February days at all and it was not until he got back to Petrograd that it seeped through to him that he was confronting a genuine people's movement not, as his suspicious mind imagined, another device for continuing the Romanov regime with a few cosmetic changes.

Lenin was not the first revolutionary to get back to Petrograd. The exiles from Siberia got there first. Among the Bolsheviks, the first group included Stalin, Lev Kamenev and Muranov. They got to Petrograd on March 12 and within a few days had pushed aside the junior Bolsheviks, Shlyapnikov, Zalutsky and a very young man named Scriabin, a nephew of the composer, who later was to became famous as Stalin's foreign minister, Viacheslav Molotov. The Siberian group took over leadership of the Party and of the Party newspaper *Pravda* and swiftly switched away from Molotov's radical line to one of support for the Provisional Government and for the war. The exiled Bolsheviks sent a telegram congratulating Grand Duke Michael on his refusal to take the throne. Stalin encountered some opposition when he came back to Petrograd. He had got on badly with his fellow exiles in Siberia and at first the Petrograd Committee voted that, because of "his inherent personal characteristics", by which was meant his rudeness, vulgarity, and selfishness, he be given only advisory membership in the Central Committee. But it took more than this to halt Stalin. Within a few days he was giving orders to those who had tried to clip his wings.

The other revolutionary leaders in Siberia returned with equal swiftness. The trains on which they rode – the Mensheviks, F. I. Dan and I. G. Tsereteli, Catherine Breshko-Breshkovsky, the Socialist Revolutionary leader and all the others – were decorated with fir boughs and red banners.

At every station there were meetings and when the exiles arrived at Moscow and Petrograd a ceremonial ritual was established. Catherine Breshko-Breshkovsky was taken for a ride in the Czar's carriage. By the time Lenin's special train pulled into Petrograd's Finland Station beside the Neva river in the Vyborg quarter at ten minutes after 11 pm on the evening of April 3, the reception procedure had become almost a stereotype.

Trotsky reviews a May Day demonstration in Palace Square, Petrograd. His son, Sereyozha, is beside him.

FACING PAGE
Leon Trotsky was second only to Lenin in the execution of the Bolshevik coup d'état and in the new Bolshevik regime. But he had not been a Bolshevik prior to his return from exile to Russia in May 1917. He held views very similar to Lenin's but the two men had been political antagonists. In partnership they worked remarkably well, but old line Party members in Bolshevik ranks never really accepted Trotsky. He was at his best in organizing and leading the Red Army in the desperate battles fought by the Reds against the White Guard armies and the Allied armies of intervention.

But Lenin broke the stereotype. He and his party had travelled from Switzerland across Germany in the famous "sealed train". It was not actually sealed but it was isolated from access on its trip across Germany. No member of Lenin's party descended from the train. Nor were any Germans permitted to meet with the Russian revolutionaries. There was one violation of this. At one station Felix Platten, a Swiss Socialist who acted as escort for the Lenin party, got off to buy some cold beer. Two German soldiers helped carry it back to the train where Karl Radek, a Polish Bolshevik, eagerly engaged the Germans in conversation until the train pulled out.

The crossing of German territory drew, as Lenin knew it would, a storm of criticism for "collusion with the enemy". The Germans were delighted to help the Bolsheviks get back to Russia since they knew Lenin wanted to pull Russia out of the war. They had, in fact, for some time been trying to encourage revolutionary movements in Russia by financial aid funnelled through an operator named Helphand (Parvus), a revolutionary adventurer who had close connections in the past with Trotsky and peripheral connections with Lenin. Some 5 million marks was made available by the German Foreign Office and Helphand syphoned it into Russia. Some of these monies reached Lenin and his Bolsheviks after his return to Russia, exactly how much has never been established, but it was enough to enable the Bolsheviks to finance their newspapers more liberally than would have otherwise been possible. This did not mean, of course, that Lenin was ever — as his enemies charged — in any sense a German agent or spy.

Lenin expected that he would be arrested the moment he arrived in Petrograd and had made arrangements with his colleagues abroad to take over if, as he feared, he was imprisoned and shot. The first question he asked the Bolshevik welcoming party at the frontier was whether he would be taken into custody when the train pulled into the Finland Station. His comrades smiled at him. His second act was to criticize the Petrograd group for the mild line it was taking in *Pravda*. The Petrograd group had suppressed a group of articles Lenin had written from Switzerland on the grounds that they were too extreme.

The Finland Station was crowded for Lenin's return. A guard of sailors from the Kronstadt naval base stood at attention and a brass band played the *Marseillaise*. Lenin spoke briefly to the sailors, warning them not to trust the Provisional Government. He called for peace, bread and land and urged the sailors to fight for the full victory of the Revolution. Then he went into the Czar's reception room where he was greeted formally by Chkheidze and given a bouquet of red roses by Alexandra Kollontai in the name of the Petrograd Bolsheviks. Chkheidze called on Lenin to join ranks with the other parties and work together for the defense of Russia.

Lenin replied as though he had heard not a word Chkheidze had uttered. He spoke against the Provisional Government, for a full-fledged Socialist revolution, not only in Russia but throughout the world. Nothing like it had been heard in Petrograd. Not only was Chkheidze taken aback. So were Lenin's Bolsheviks. They hardly knew what to think.

Lenin was hoisted onto an armored car and paraded under the glare of searchlights from the Peter and Paul Fortress to the mansion of the ballerina Kshesinskaya which the Bolsheviks had requisitioned as their Party headquarters. There from the second floor balcony Lenin and other Bolshevik orators spoke to the throngs.

Lenin's talk was strong medicine for the Bolshevik Party members as well as the public. Lenin's first fight on getting back home was with his Party, to drag it, push it, shove it into the front line of the struggle as he saw it. As Shlyapnikov, one of Lenin's Petrograd lieutenants put it: "The position of Vladimir Ilyich was left of our left."

Lenin seemed to be ready to lead his party into the streets for an instant coup against the Provisional Government. But the Party was not prepared to move so fast and in such a radical direction. The Bolsheviks carried out two abortive street demonstrations in April, which only aroused deep suspicion on the part of the other left-wing parties that Lenin was prepared to seize power by whatever means came to hand.

Meantime, Lenin strengthened his forces, prepared plans, won adherents. One of the most important to rally to Lenin was Leon Trotsky. Trotsky was the last important revolutionary to get back to Russia. He was held up by the British and put in a con-

centration camp outside Halifax, Nova Scotia. It was May before he and his family arrived in Petrograd. Trotsky and Lenin joined forces and within six weeks Trotsky became a full-fledged Bolshevik and number two in the Party – after Lenin. The old-line Bolsheviks accepted Trotsky as an ally but strongly mistrusted him as a rival, a mistrust which was never to be lost and was ultimately to play a major role in the history of the Bolsheviks and in that of Russia and the world.

Revolution hardly took Russia's poets and artists by surprise. They, long before the politicians, had sensed the coming of the storm. And they, more than anyone except a few police specialists, understood that this was no orderly, conspiratorial movement but a convulsion starting within the dark masses of the people, a whirlwind which swept in from the broad Russian steppe, overwhelmed the cities and ravaged the countryside. It was, they knew, an elemental force which made its own rules, toppling centuries-old institutions, smashing principles and theories as a tidal wave crushes ships against a jetty, heedless of individuals, impossible to tame, as pervasive as a flood and as devastating as a forest fire.

There was, they knew, much in the 1917 Revolution of the extremism of ancient peasant cults, the fire-worshippers who locked themselves in wooden churches and perished as flames devoured the structure, the orgiasts who drank, smashed, looted, copulated, fought until intoxication and exhaustion laid everyone low, some killed, some wounded, some dead drunk.

Maxim Gorky, the most radical of Russian writers, was cautious in his attitude toward the Revolution. He doubted that it would last, feared the peasant-soldiers, thought clashes with the workers inevitable and doubted that the regime could survive. He did, however, start a newspaper and invited other writers and poets to contribute.

One contributor was Vladimir Mayakovsky. This poet didn't bother to try to understand the Revolution. He simply embraced it. He ran through the streets wherever there was firing and dashed off revolutionary verse like bursts from a machine gun. He was in love with the violence. Andrei Bely, the poet and mystic, could hardly write, so obsessed was he by events at the Tauride Palace. His great friend, the poet Alexander Blok, put himself at the service of the special commission investigating the Czarist regime and plunged into the writing of a history of the period leading up to the February events. Zinaida Gippius, a remarkable diarist and mistress of Petrograd's most fashionable literary salon, devoted herself to Kerensky whom she profoundly mistrusted, but whose incessant activity engaged her attention. Later, the flamboyant Socialist Revolutionary terrorist Boris Savinkov returned to Petrograd and Gippius watched his complex intrigues with despair and amazement. Gippius' husband,

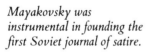

Mayakovsky was instrumental in founding the first Soviet journal of satire.

One of Rodchenko's most striking photomontages — created for Vladimir Mayakovsky's poem, "About This". Mayakovsky worked closely with Rodchenko and the Constructivists.

Dmitri Merezhkovsky, continued his religious-philosophical writing until he was diverted by Kerensky's demands that he write pamphlets.

No one in these first revolutionary days wrote or painted anything memorable. The pace was too fast, the atmosphere too hectic. The artists found themselves so caught up in each day they had no time to transform their impressions into poetry or art. Ivan Bunin, (later, in exile, to win the Nobel prize for literature), went to luncheons and banquets at which writers and poets gave addresses about the necessity of preserving Russia's cultural heritage. Artists like Benois, Roerich, Larionov, the singer Chaliapin, the theatrical director Meyerhold and the composer Sergei Prokofiev, joined in grandiose socio-cultural projects, none of which left a trace in the historical record.

Now that the events which they had so long predicted had finally come to pass it was as though the poets had lost their voices, the artists' their brushes, the composers their musical sense. It was, in fact, a time for participation. Not for celebration.

OVERLEAF
On July 3, 1917 widespread rioting broke out in Petrograd as left-wing forces associated with Lenin's Bolshevik faction demonstrated in what was widely regarded as the initial phase of a coup d'état. This is a scene on the Nevsky Prospekt, the main thoroughfare of Petrograd.

CHAPTER 10

This May Day call sends greetings to all the workers of Russia.

ДА ЗДРАВСТВУЕТ ПРАЗДНИК ТРУДЯЩИХСЯ ВСЕХ СТРАН!

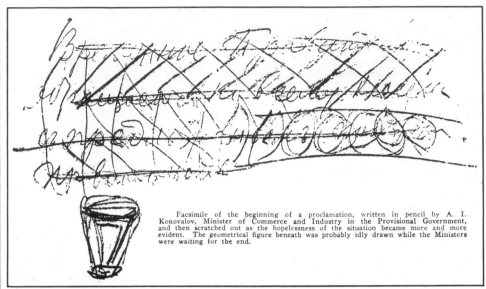

Facsimile of the beginning of a proclamation, written in pencil by A. I. Konovalov, Minister of Commerce and Industry in the Provisional Government, and then scratched out as the hopelessness of the situation became more and more evident. The geometrical figure beneath was probably idly drawn while the Ministers were waiting for the end.

The Provisional Government was soon involved in a series of crises. Minister after minister dropped from sight. With the departure of Guchkov and Milyukov, Kerensky became Minister of Defense. Now he was constantly on the go, travelling from one front to another, attempting by every trick of the tongue to keep Russia's armies in the field, to maintain a front against the Germans and even, in June, to launch a major offensive. It was a virtuoso performance. The Russian armies were being bled white, not by German arms, but by desertion. Every day thousands of peasant soldiers slipped away by foot or on the encumbered trains back to their native villages. There was no improvement in supplies. The production of munitions went down as factories fell more and more into disarray. Under provisions of "Order No. 1" issued by the Soviet it was almost impossible for officers to enforce discipline since they had lost the ordinary rights to punish or compel soldiers to carry out orders against their personal wishes.

Despite these handicaps Kerensky organized an offensive which was designed to begin in mid-June with an attack by the Southwest Army. This army was headed by the extremely competent General Brusilov. Brusilov was named by Kerensky to replace General Alekseev, the Czar's old Chief of Staff who had been acting as Commander-in-Chief at Mogilev. Later Brusilov was to take service under the Bolsheviks in the Red Army. The offensive under Brusilov's general direction, with Kerensky looking on, started out well. The attack was taken up by General Kornilov's 8th Army and this was intended to be followed by an advance on the part of General Denikin's Western Front.

But in the end Kerensky's offensive achieved no military results. The push forward petered out and was quickly followed by new German pressures. But the initial successes led to political gains for Kerensky and setbacks for Lenin. On June 10 the Bolsheviks had been on the verge of another test of strength in the streets. Whether Lenin hoped to seize power through the demonstration has never been determined. Lenin called off the test at the last moment and Trotsky always denied that the Bolsheviks had any intention of a coup.

But Petrograd grew more jittery and in late June radical Bolsheviks and Anarchists began to prepare for another attempt. Lenin's role in this coup is also murky. He had gone into the Finnish countryside for a rest when the crisis erupted on July 4. He rushed back to Petrograd where the situation swiftly began to change. The Soviet brought in loyal troops from outside the city and rumors swept Petrograd that documents had been uncovered showing that Lenin was a "German Agent". The "evidence" was something less than conclusive, but it was enough to turn the tide. Lenin went underground. The *Pravda* plant was smashed by troops. The Kshesinskaya mansion was occupied. The Provisional Government issued warrants for the arrest of Lenin, Trotsky, Zinoviev, Kamenev and Lunacharsky. "They're getting ready to shoot

134

American troops participated in the intervention against the Bolsheviks on the Northern Front, debarking at Archangel, and also in Siberia, landing in Vladivostok and moving west along the Trans-Siberian railroad. Here Americans guard Russian prisoners at Archangel.

us, aren't they," Lenin said to Trotsky. Lenin decided to turn himself in but at the last moment the Central Committee persuaded him to change his mind and go into hiding.

Disguised as a locomotive engineer, Lenin made his way to Finland where he set up in exile as a hay maker. Kerensky took the helm of the Provisional Government as Prime Minister.

It was an unhappy summer for Russia. Conditions at the front deteriorated week by week. Conditions in the countryside deteriorated even more rapidly. Landlord after landlord was driven from his estates. Not a few were murdered. Manor houses were put to the torch. Crops burned in the fields. Animals were slaughtered. The peasants took the land. They did not wait for anyone's permission or decree. They pillaged the great farms. Many would never again be so productive. Railroad services began to fall apart. Troops at the front simply requisitioned trains and forced the engineers to take them to the rear. It became more and more difficult to get supplies to the front. The cities began to suffer. In the countryside peasants found it harder and harder to get salt, kerosene, cotton goods, shoes, leather and nails. Factories in Petrograd, Moscow and the other great cities fell idle. The workers were out making the revolution and there were no parts for the machines nor raw materials for manufacture.

Cabs and horse-drawn carriages began to disappear. Streetcar service was erratic. The railroad stations filled with vagrants and deserting soldiers, often drunk, sometimes threatening. The police force had vanished in the first days of the Revolution. Now "revolutionary order" was disintegrating. Holdups and robberies became the order of the day.

Politically, signs of deterioration were everywhere. Kerensky moved into the Winter Palace and slept in the Czar's bed, but most of the time he was whirling about the country, his frenzy and oratory less and less effective. In late July he sent Nicholas II, Alexandra and their family, now almost forgotten by their one-time subjects, to the remote, old, backward Siberian city of Tobolsk. The Czar had hoped that he and his family would be allowed to take refuge in England. But the Provisional Government did not act in its first days of power and soon the more radical Soviet began objecting to the idea of letting the Imperial family go abroad. And, more important, the British Government and King George V, Nicholas' cousin, had second thoughts. They privately advised the Russians that the Romanovs were no longer welcome. They could have been sent to neutral Denmark or France but nothing was done. Now, possibly because Kerensky feared some harm might come to the Imperial family, or possibly as a political gesture to show that he, too, could be harsh toward the Czar, he secretly arranged to send them to Siberia. The move was undertaken quietly and the family settled

OVERLEAF
Youngsters were sent to camps and given training in calisthenics and even military drill, as one of the short-lived social reforms of the Provisional Government.

Fraternization became more common than combat at the front. Here an Austrian and a Russian soldier exchange cigarettes.

down to a dull but not uncomfortable existence. Tobolsk was a very conservative town, hardly touched by the Revolution. The Czar had plenty of opportunity for physical exercise. He spent much time chopping wood and organized informal classes so that the five children could continue their education.

The next big crisis came at the end of August. It was a complex affair in which Kerensky, General Kornilov and the famous Socialist Revolutionary adventurer, Boris Savinkov, participated. It was rumored – but never proved – that the British Ambassador, Sir George Buchanan, a forthright, no-nonsense man whose only objective was to ensure that Russia remained in the war, was involved.

Kornilov was a bluff military man. One of his colleagues said he had the heart of a lion and the brains of a sheep. His own objective was quite clear: to make himself dictator of Russia, overthrow the revolution and install a military regime. He probably would not have put Nicholas II back on his throne but he might have opened the way to some kind of Romanov restoration. He was the first of what was to prove a succession of ambitious military adventurers bent on seizing power, but neither his intentions nor his strategy were well conceived. Kornilov hoped to march on Petrograd with front-line troops and take the capital in a single move. It did not work out that way because Kerensky (who had named Kornilov Commander-in-Chief) was playing his own game and so was the adventurer Boris Savinkov. Each, in fact, thought he could use the others to win a struggle for supremacy.

All were disappointed. Kerensky had to turn to the Soviet for help to halt Kornilov's march on Petrograd. The Soviet had to turn for help to the Bolshevik military organization. The Bolsheviks responded with enthusiasm, organized substantial forces and with little trouble succeeded in turning back Kornilov's offensive and compelling the general to flee for his life. Kerensky managed to hang onto his tottering regime but the Bolshevik military organization acquired large stocks of arms, ammunition and experience – all of which it would shortly put to its own use.

Kerensky's "victory" was to prove short-lived.

Kerensky survived but he had placed a fatal mortgage on his power. He retained it only thanks to the military support of the Bolsheviks. As the sharp-witted Zinadia Gippius put it: "Kerensky is now completely in the hands of the maximalists and the Bolsheviks."

She exaggerated a little but not much. Lenin was still in deep cover, hiding in Finland, living for a while with the Chief of Police of Helsingfors who happened to be a Communist. But the Party organization had recovered from the trauma of July. Lenin was absolutely certain that events were now moving in a direction which would lead the Bolsheviks to power. His colleagues were not so certain. They were more cautious and conservative than their leader.

There were many signs that events were playing into the hands of the Bolsheviks. As Count de Robien, the observant French diplomat, noted: "The parties of disorder profit by the situation and hope to impose a Bolshevik government...it is the decisive moment for the Russian revolution."

The Bolsheviks began to show new strength in local elections. On August 20 they won 33 percent of the vote for the Petrograd City Duma against 20 percent in May. On the night of September 1-2 they won a majority in the Petrograd Soviet. On September 5 they won in the Moscow Soviet and on September 9 the Bolsheviks mustered 519 votes to their opponents' 414, with 67 abstentions, on a key vote in the Petrograd Soviet. Trotsky took over chairmanship of the Petrograd Soviet.

A week later the Bolsheviks crushed the opposition in the vote for the district Duma in Moscow, winning 52 percent. Some military units voted better than 90 percent for the Bolsheviks.

The British Ambassador frankly concluded that if the Government was not strong enough to put down the Bolsheviks by force (and Buchanan was convinced they were not) the only alternative, and a disastrous one, would be a Bolshevik government.

This, essentially, was Lenin's assessment and he now set about seizing power. He was not to deviate from that objective until it had been attained.

CHAPTER 11

Russian women on the streets of Petrograd, 1917.

n Petrograd there was a strong sense of time running out. This was felt by all of the observers. Count de Robien thought that, underlying the maneuvering of politicians and revolutionaries, there was in Russia a tremendous war weariness shared by everyone – the soldiers, the peasants, the ordinary citizens. If the country was to be saved from even more violent revolution peace must be made with Germany. The whole of Russia, de Robien felt, had arrived at this conviction.

Kerensky continued to maneuver politically. He called a conference to prepare the way for Russia's long-awaited national elections for a Constituent Assembly which would establish a full-fledged democratic government. But the meeting went badly. Kerensky had lost touch with reality. He was giving himself the airs of a dictator.

"It is perhaps for the best," de Robien remarked, "that the crisis should come to a head as soon as possible and that the abscess should burst as it is inevitable anyway."

Ambassador Buchanan kept stressing to Kerensky that Bolshevism was the root of all the "evils from which Russia was suffering". He told Kerensky that if he would smash Bolshevism he would go down in history as the savior of his country. Kerensky said he could not move until the Bolsheviks rose. Then he would step in and wipe them out. Kerensky anticipated an armed rising by the Bolsheviks in "the next few weeks". It was mid-October when he expressed that opinion.

Kerensky was close to the mark. All through September, Lenin belabored his Petrograd associates with one fiery letter after another from his Finnish hideout. He abandoned Helsingfors and moved to Vyborg on the Finnish-Russian frontier line to communicate more rapidly with Petrograd.

Lenin insisted that the time had come for armed insurrection in Petrograd and Moscow; that the majority of Russians now sided with the Bolsheviks; that the Provisional Government might surrender Petrograd to the Germans; that the time for action was *now*. He spelled out his views in two letters to his colleagues in mid-September. They did not agree with him. In fact, they seem to have thought Lenin had lost touch with reality. They ordered his letters buried in the Party archives and banned any kind of revolutionary action. For while the Petrograd Bolsheviks agreed with Lenin that things were moving in their direction, they did not think the game had reached the stage of all or nothing. They believed power would flow naturally into their hands when the All-Russian Soviet convened on October 20. With victory so close they saw no reason for Lenin's wild excitement.

This reasoning drove Lenin to frenzy. He foresaw all kinds of evil consequences. The British might make a separate peace with the Germans, the countryside was already in revolt and the Bolsheviks would miss the psychological moment, Finland was about to rise, the Ukraine might detach itself from Russia, the Cossacks might be mobilized against Petrograd. There was no end to his arguments.

Finally on September 29, Lenin sent a letter tendering his resignation from the Central Committee in order to carry his campaign for a *coup d'etat* directly to the Party membership. He also opened up a correspondence with leaders of the Finnish Communist movement about using Finnish troops and naval forces to seize power.

At some time during this period Lenin slipped back into Petrograd and went to a secret hiding place in the apartment of a woman agronomist named Fofanova. There is much evidence that he returned without permission of the Central Committee and against its orders. For many years, particularly in the Stalin period, the evidence of Lenin's violent controversy with his colleagues over the uprising was concealed in Party archives. Even today the facts are not all known.

In any event, by late September or early October Lenin was back in Petrograd and the Central Committee began slowly to move in the direction of his wishes. On October 10 the Central Committee approved an armed uprising but still fixed no date.

By this time Petrograd buzzed with rumors that the Bolsheviks planned an armed move. All through late September gossip flourished and the newspapers published declarations that the Bolsheviks had fixed October 20 as the date for their move. The reports, in fact, were somewhat ahead of events. The idea of a Bolshevik uprising was accepted as fact by many of Petrograd's citizens before Lenin had managed to convince a majority of the Central Committee to carry it out.

And even after Lenin's victory of October 10 there was another big argument on the 15th. Lenin had the firm support of fifteen of the twenty-five members present but an important faction of the Party centered around two of the most prominent members, Kamenev and Zinoviev. They felt the uprising would be a disaster.

Lenin won again on the 15th (although a date for the rising was not yet fixed). But Zinoviev and Kamenev would not be stilled. They carried their fight into public and on the 17th Maxim Gorky's newspaper published an article declaring that the Bolsheviks were preparing a coup and that two leading members had dissented from the decision. The next day a public declaration was made by Kamenev dissenting from the decision. Lenin flew into a fit of temper. He, too, took to the press and denounced Kamenev and Zinoviev.

Thus, the plans for the uprising moved forward in the full spotlight of public attention. Far from being a secret conspiracy the "plot" was the subject of every conversation in Petrograd. Each edition of the newspapers gave more details.

This did not deter Lenin. His attitude was that they must go full speed ahead. He wanted to throw Kamenev and Zinoviev out of the party. But even in this he did not

Kasimir Malevich's 1912 construction; The Knife-Grinder, *represents his Futurist attempt to confront the problem of man and the machine. He catches them at a moment in time and space. There is no movement, rather an arrest of movement. Man dominates the machine.*

succeed. The men were merely reprimanded and ordered to stop campaigning against the Party's decisions. Stalin opposed this mild reprimand and resigned from the editorial board of the Party newspaper, *Rabochy Put*. His resignation was refused.

What were Kerensky and his Government doing during these days?

Warnings had been sent to garrisons around the country to be on the alert. The sale of revolvers without a permit was banned (but only after everyone in Petrograd, it seemed, was carrying one). Lenin's arrest was ordered but not that of Trotsky. Kerensky and the Petrograd commandant assured foreign diplomats that the Petrograd troops were totally reliable and would support the Government. Kerensky told those who questioned him that he could hardly wait for the Bolsheviks to start because this would give him an opportunity to mop them up. He did not bother to order additional troops into the capital but he did set up a few guard posts on the approaches to the Winter Palace. He brought some military cadets and bicycle squads in to supplement the regular Palace guard. By October 22 the Palace was protected by a force of about 800 equipped with six field guns, six armored cars and nineteen machineguns.

Bolshevik plans for the coup went forward lackadaisically. The Military Revolutionary Committee of the Soviet was employed as a cover organization. Ostensibly the Bolsheviks, through the Committee, were preparing to defend the Soviet against any attempt by Kerensky or the military to attack it.

So confident was the Petrograd Commandant, Colonel Polkovnikov, of his control over the situation that when delegates of the Military Revolutionary Committee told him they had authority to supervise any orders he might issue and were sending in three Commissars to countersign his orders, the Colonel quietly told them he would

Въ БОРЬБѢ ОБРѢТЕШЬ ТЫ ПРАВО СВОЕ

ДОЛОЙ МОНАРХІЮ ЗДРАВСТВУЕТ РЕСПУБЛИКА

not accept the Commissars and provided a car to take them back to Smolny, the former residence of a school for noblewomen, where the Soviet had set up headquarters. The MRC delegates were so astounded by Polkovnikov's self-confidence that they did not protest. But when they got back to Smolny they issued instructions to the Petrograd garrison not to obey any orders which they had not countersigned.

Nikolai Sukhanov, the great diarist of the Revolution, felt that this confrontation marked the start of the *coup d'état*. Except that neither Polkovnikov nor the MRC realized it. Thus, the dispute between Polkovnikov and the MRC led not to rebellion but to efforts to find a compromise. When Lenin heard about this he flew into a rage. Kerensky paid no attention whatever.

Another matter which bothered Lenin was the fact that no date or hour had yet been set for the uprising. He was still in hiding in Fofanova's apartment, his communications with the Central Committee were erratic and, in spite of the great row, his opponents Zinoviev and Kamenev were hard at work with the other Bolsheviks at Smolny as though nothing had happened.

Anger and energy spent, Lenin now seemed to sink into a kind of lethargy. So far as the record goes he did little or nothing from the 20th to the 23rd of October.

His colleagues were moving by fits and starts. On Saturday, October 21 the Bolsheviks won control of the Petrograd Cartridge Factory. This gave them access to unlimited ammunition. It also meant the Government could get shells and bullets only if the MRC approved the order.

An impartial investigation after the Bolshevik coup reported that no member of the Women's Battalion had been raped, none were killed, none were wounded. One woman committed suicide but this seemed to have no connection with her military service.

Sunday October 22 was a day of tension. Soviet meetings and parades had been scheduled for almost every quarter of Petrograd. At the same time the Cossack regiments planned a great religious procession. There was every likelihood of a collision. But the Bolsheviks and Government did their utmost to prevent the confrontation. They managed to persuade the Cossacks not to take to the streets. Thus, the possibility of an armed seizure of Petrograd by the Bolsheviks on Sunday was averted, in part, through Bolshevik collaboration.

Monday the 23rd was a cold raw day. De Robien reported the city in ferment and anticipated an outbreak at any moment. Ambassador Buchanan heard that the Bolsheviks were about to carry out their coup but Foreign Minister Tereshchenko told him the reports were not true and that the Government had matters well in hand. John Reed, the American socialist and correspondent, visited Smolny that evening and found it a beehive of activity. One Bolshevik waved a revolver at him and declared, "The game is on!"

Kerensky met with his ministers in the Czar's quarters of the Winter Palace. Negotiations were going on between the Government and the MRC trying to work out some compromise under which relations between the two bodies and the armed forces could be regularized. The talks went on through the evening and apparently were still in progress in the early hours of the 24th but nothing was decided.

The night of October 23-24 was miserable and windy. John Reed thought Petrograd was unusually nervous. He noticed that the city militia had been issued with new revolvers in raw leather holsters. Lights burned late at Smolny Institute but exactly what was happening no one seemed to know. Lenin was still in hiding at Fofanova's apartment. The Bolsheviks were trying to persuade troops of the Petrograd garrison to come over to their side but the men were not interested in anything, certainly not in fighting. At midnight the electricity in Petrograd was turned off as a conservation measure but cabarets, houses of prostitution and gambling halls kept their lights on by paying bribes.

Rather late in the evening Kerensky ordered some more troops into the city — a regiment from Tsarskoye Selo, a company of cadets, an artillery battery and the First Women's Battalion. A fistful of edicts was issued ordering citizens to put automobiles at the disposition of the Government, instructing military units to obey only orders issued by the Army Command, removing the Petrograd Soviet commissars and launching an investigation of illegal acts.

At about 3 am Kerensky cut off telephone service to Smolny and a bit later a detachment of cadets raided *Rabochy Put,* the Bolshevik paper, confiscated the newspaper and sealed the plant. Then they did the same thing to *Novoye Rus* and *Zhivoye Slovo,* right-wing newspapers.

It did not take the Bolsheviks long to get telephone service restored to Smolny and within a few hours they had *Rabochy Put* operating again.

During the night the first steps were taken to strengthen defenses at Smolny, the

Bolshevik headquarters. (Up to this time Smolny had been guarded with troops provided by Kerensky.) Machineguns were mounted, reliable troops brought in, barricades of firewood thrown up and cannon placed at the entrance.

Tuesday the 24th passed like some kind of hallucination. The ever-observant Count de Robien reported: "In spite of our fears for today, everything has been quiet. Besides, the Government has taken precautions and raised some troops who are believed to be reliable."

David Francis, the bumbling St Louis politician who was serving in Petrograd as US Minister, visited Foreign Minister Tereshchenko who told him a Bolshevik uprising was expected that evening. Tereshchenko was looking forward to the uprising. He was certain the Government could suppress it.

Kerensky took several minor precautions. He ordered detachments of troops to the telephone office, the post office and telegraph offices. Cadet patrols were sent into the streets to set up traffic controls. In mid-afternoon three of the four principal bridges across the Neva were raised. This spread nervousness through the city. Minor scuffles between Government troops and Bolshevik detachments broke out but no blood was shed. The Government retained control of some bridges, the Bolsheviks took over others.

Kerensky decided to unlimber his principal weapon – his oratory. A pre-parliamentary meeting was in progress, designed to pave the way for the forthcoming Constituent Assembly. Kerensky presented himself before the politicians and made a dramatic speech. His Government, he said, had worked out a plan for turning over the land to the peasants. He was sending a delegation to Paris to meet with the French and British on war aims. He promised a fight to the death to defend the Provisional Government and warned that part of the Petrograd garrison was in a state of insurgency. He called Lenin a state criminal and announced a judicial inquiry into his conduct and that of the Bolsheviks.

Kerensky won an ovation, but not the vote of confidence he needed. The Pre-Parliament condemned the Bolsheviks for their impending revolt but blamed Kerensky for the conditions which had given rise to it. It called for an immediate grant of land to the peasants and immediate peace. It decided to take into its own hands the task of combatting the Bolshevik uprising once it got underway.

By the end of Kerensky's appearance it was apparent that, regardless of what the Bolsheviks did, he and his Government were finished.

The Bolsheviks did little this day. They persuaded some troops to ignore Kerensky's orders and not come into Petrograd and they got the bicycle troops to abandon their guard posts at the Winter Palace. That was about all. In fact, the conservative newspaper, *Rech,* reported that up to 10 pm nothing serious had happened. There had been no military clashes anywhere in the city.

Young Russian cadets (junkers) guarding the Winter Palace. Behind them are barricades made of firewood.

OVERLEAF
The Bolsheviks brought in sailors from the Kronstadt naval base and the Baltic Fleet to augment their revolutionary forces in Petrograd.

CHAPTER 12

This proclamation, written by Lenin, was plastered up on the walls of Petrograd on October 26. It announced the fall of the Provisional Government and said that power had passed into the hands of the Petrograd Soviet and the Military Revolutionary Committee (controlled by the Bolsheviks). At the time the proclamation was put up the Provisional Government was still operating in Petrograd.

Къ Гражданамъ Россіи.

Временное Правительство низложено. Государственная власть перешла въ руки органа Петроградскаго Совѣта Рабочихъ и Солдатскихъ Депутатовъ Военно-Революціоннаго Комитета, стоящаго во главѣ Петроградскаго пролетаріата и гарнизона.

Дѣло, за которое боролся народъ: немедленное предложеніе демократическаго мира, отмѣна помѣщичьей собственности на землю, рабочій контроль надъ производствомъ, созданіе Совѣтскаго Правительства — это дѣло обезпечено.

ДА ЗДРАВСТВУЕТЪ РЕВОЛЮЦІЯ РАБОЧИХЪ, СОЛДАТЪ И КРЕСТЬЯНЪ!

Военно-Революціонный Комитетъ
при Петроградскомъ Совѣтѣ
Рабочихъ и Солдатскихъ Депутатовъ.

25 октября 1917 г. 10 ч. утра.

Posters went up in the cities, trying to arouse people to the crisis. The starving figures of peasants cried: "Help!"

All through Tuesday Lenin waited alone in the Fofanova apartment on the Vyborg side where he had been living since returning to Petrograd. He was isolated from the Central Committee at the Smolny Institute. Bolshevik historians claim that he was in touch with the Committee by courier during the day, frequently exchanging notes, reports and instructions. This may be true but none of these communications have survived. What is positively known is that Fofanova got back to her flat around 5 pm and told Lenin that alarming rumors were circulating in Petrograd and that the Neva bridges had been raised. Lenin rushed to his room, dashed off a note and asked Fofanova to deliver it immediately to his wife, Nadezhda Krupskaya, to be passed on to his comrades. He told Fofanova that it was necessary to get on with the uprising this very evening — there could be no more temporizing, and he should be at Smolny.

In the letter he declared that "the situation is critical in the extreme" and that further delay in the uprising would be fatal. The Provisional Government was tottering and "it must be given the death blow at all costs." (Lenin himself underlined the phrase.) He didn't care how it was done — so long as it was done immediately.

There are some questions about the letter. Most Soviet histories say Lenin sent it to the Party Central Committee at Smolny. In fact, however, it is now known the letter was addressed to the regional Party Committees, not the Central Committee. Lenin had despaired of action by the Central Committee and once again was going over the heads of the Party leadership and taking his case to the membership itself.

Lenin exchanged several notes with Krupskaya that evening. The texts of none of these notes have ever been published. Nor has anyone offered a logical explanation why Lenin did not simply join his colleagues at Smolny, nor why they did not urgently summon him. Whatever the explanation, Lenin finally scribbled a message to Fofanova saying: "I've gone where you didn't want me to go," and set off for Smolny with a man named Rahja, a Finn who had accompanied him during his days in hiding in Finland.

Lenin and Rahja made their way across Petrograd on foot and by streetcar and despite an encounter or two with patrols arrived safely at Smolny not long before 11 pm. With Lenin's arrival the pace of events gradually began to quicken. But no time-table for the uprising was ever agreed upon.

After addressing the Pre-Parliament Alexander Kerensky went back to the Winter Palace and sat down with his colleagues in the famous Malachite Chamber with its green Urals stone columns and fireplaces, its malachite tables and vases. The Palace was something of a shambles. Many of its furnishings and the famous works of art from the Hermitage had been packed for shipment to Moscow because of fears that advancing German troops might capture Petrograd. A large portion of the Palace was occupied by a hospital as convalescent quarters for the wounded and another section was being used as barracks for the small defense force.

Kerensky met with his ministers until about 2 am when they wearily made their ways home, leaving Kerensky nervous and distraught. He and his deputy Konovalev went across Palace Square to the General Staff building after the others had departed. They stayed there until about 7 am issuing orders to troops to come to the defense of Petrograd (none of the units ever appeared). Then they returned to the Winter Palace. It was a dark cold morning and Kerensky lay down on his bed, which once had been used by Nicholas II, for a little rest. He rose at 9 am to find his telephone dead. Pulling back the heavy curtains he saw the sun just rising and discovered that the Palace bridge over the Neva was now in the hands of the Bolsheviks.

Kerensky decided he could not remain a moment longer. He must leave the capital, round up some reliable troops from the front and return to save the situation. The decision was easier to make than to carry out because all of the cars in the Palace courtyard had been disabled by Bolshevik chauffeurs. Finally Kerensky managed to borrow a Renault belonging to the American embassy and a Pierce-Arrow from some other source, possibly the British. With the Renault in front, flying an American flag, Kerensky sat in the open Pierce-Arrow, raced through the heart of Petrograd and out of town to Gatchina and Pskov to try to rally troops to his side.

Color Poster by V. Lebedev for ROSTA, the State Telegraph Agency, to be used in window propaganda display.

Lenin was now in charge at Smolny. He had been up most of the night exhorting his colleagues, consulting members of the Military Revolutionary Committee, making certain that *this time* the coup would really get going. About 10 am he drafted a proclamation and Bolshevik trucks rushed through Petrograd, plastering it on the city walls. John Reed, the young American, saw it when he emerged rather late in the morning from the Hotel Astoria where he was staying with his girl friend, Louise Bryant. It said:

To the Citizens of Russia!

The Provisional Government has been deposed. State power has passed into the hands of the organ of the Petrograd Soviet of Workers and Soldiers Deputies – the Revolutionary Military Committee, which heads the Petrograd proletariat and the garrison.

The cause for which the people have fought, namely, the immediate offer of a democratic peace, the abolition of landed proprietorship, workers' control over production and the establishment of Soviet power – this cause has been secured.

Long live the revolution of workers, soldiers and peasants!

Actually, the Provisional Government had not been deposed. Not at this hour. It still existed. The Bolsheviks had taken over a good part of the central section of Petrograd. But not the Mariinsky Palace where the Pre-Parliament was still meeting, not the City Duma (and City Administration), not the War Ministry across from St Isaac's Cathedral in the city's heart, not the Winter Palace and, of course, not the country nor

Barricades were being thrown
up in the Petrograd streets.
The Revolution was in full
swing.

its military forces and staff headquarters still engaged in combat (rather listless to be sure) with the Germans along the 1,200-mile front.

The truth was that the streets of Petrograd were perfectly quiet. There was none of the rampaging about town by trucks loaded with grim and picturesque soldiers which had marked earlier crises. True, a few dozen Bolshevik troops did visit the Mariinsky Palace in the early afternoon and closed down the session of the Pre-Parliament. Louise Bryant was there when it happened. A big Kronstadt sailor (the Bolsheviks had brought several thousand sailors from Kronstadt and the Baltic fleet into Petrograd) simply marched into the red-and-gold assembly hall and announced: "No more Council. Go along home!" The members docilely filed out and the Bolsheviks didn't even bother to arrest them.

A picket line of junkers, young cadets from training schools, had been strung out in front of the Winter Palace but neither they nor a similar picket line of Bolshevik soldiers and red guards which appeared in the Square a little later made much fuss about letting people through. By mid-afternoon a dozen or more newsmen including Claude Anet, a French correspondent, John Reed and Louise Bryant, and reporters for the Petrograd press had got into the Winter Palace.

There in the Malachite Chamber, so symbolic of the old Russian order, Kerensky's Ministers had gathered for a last stand. They were only gradually becoming aware of the control the Bolsheviks now exercised in Petrograd. The Bolsheviks held the telephone exchange, the post office and telegraph station, the railroad stations and most of the public buildings. Except for the Winter Palace itself – a vast complex spreading for a half mile along the Neva river – and the facing General Staff building with its grandiose arch, the Bolsheviks had, in fact, taken over the city. But neither the Provisional Ministers nor the Bolsheviks quite realized this. Lenin's nerves were growing jagged. He kept insisting that the Winter Palace be taken. The Soviet was meeting that afternoon at Smolny and he wanted to announce the fall of the Palace. Without that his Proclamation seemed a bit wobbly. The Military Revolutionary Committee made promises but nothing happened. It was after 1 pm by the time they managed to close down the Pre-Parliament in the Mariinsky Palace (and they completely forgot about taking over the War Ministry; not until 6 pm did Bolsheviks appear there). Telephone service to the Winter Palace was supposedly cut off but actually a number of lines remained open and the Ministers used them, calling Staff Headquarters at Mogilev, telephoning to various Party headquarters in town, to the City Duma, to prominent citizens, trying to drum up support. They kept hoping some of the Cossack troops would come to their aid but only a handful turned up. None of the Petrograd troops wanted to get involved.

The afternoon wore by. Petrograd's shops stayed open. Streetcars jangled past. Shoppers queued up at the butchers and bakers. Except for Lenin's proclamation there was no sign anything unusual was underway. Nowhere were there armed collisions. Nowhere did revolutionary combat break out.

Lenin finally made his speech to the Soviet at Smolny. He simply ignored the Winter Palace and repeated his proclamation of the morning. The Military Revolutionary Committee worked out a plan of action. The Winter Palace would be sent an ultimatum to surrender. If it refused a red lantern would be hoisted on the tower of the Peter and Paul Fortress. The cruiser *Aurora* would fire a blank round from its six-inch guns and the assault on the Winter Palace would be on.

Louise Bryant felt sorry for the young cadets who were defending the Winter Palace. They were mostly teenagers. ("Children" was what the French correspondent Claude Anet called them.) They fiddled with their guns and one swore he was keeping the last bullet for himself. His comrades chimed in that they were doing the same. Some exchanged souvenirs with Louise Bryant. She remembered getting a ring with an inscription from the Czar and a Caucasian dagger worked in silver. Outside in the Square a busy little man with a box camera set up a tripod, put his head under a black cloth and began to take pictures of the junkers and the Women's Battalion lugging logs from the Kremlin's winter heating supply and hoisting them up into barricades before the main Palace entrance.

In the Malachite Chamber the Ministers got a promise from Mogilev Staff head-

quarters that if they could hold out 48 hours reinforcements would be sent. Some of the Palace defenders began to trickle away including a Cossack detachment that clattered out of the Palace courtyard on horseback, leaving behind its machineguns after a big argument. More and more Bolsheviks infiltrated the Winter Palace, coming in through undefended entrances (there were several hundred doors to the huge complex). Most of the infiltrators permitted themselves to be taken into custody without argument but their sheer numbers began to raise the question of whether the handful of defenders would not be swamped by their "prisoners".

Events resembled a theater of the absurd. The Military Revolutionary Committee couldn't find a red lantern to give the signal for the bombardment to start. The guns

In the winter of 1918 Alexander Blok wrote the great poem of the Revolution, "The Twelve", twelve peasant Red Guards marching through Petrograd in the snow, shooting and killing at random. Yuri Annenkov drew this picture for the first edition of "The Twelve".

Members of the Women's Battalion had their heads shaved or hair cut short, not to make them look masculine, but because of the danger of lice which carried typhus.

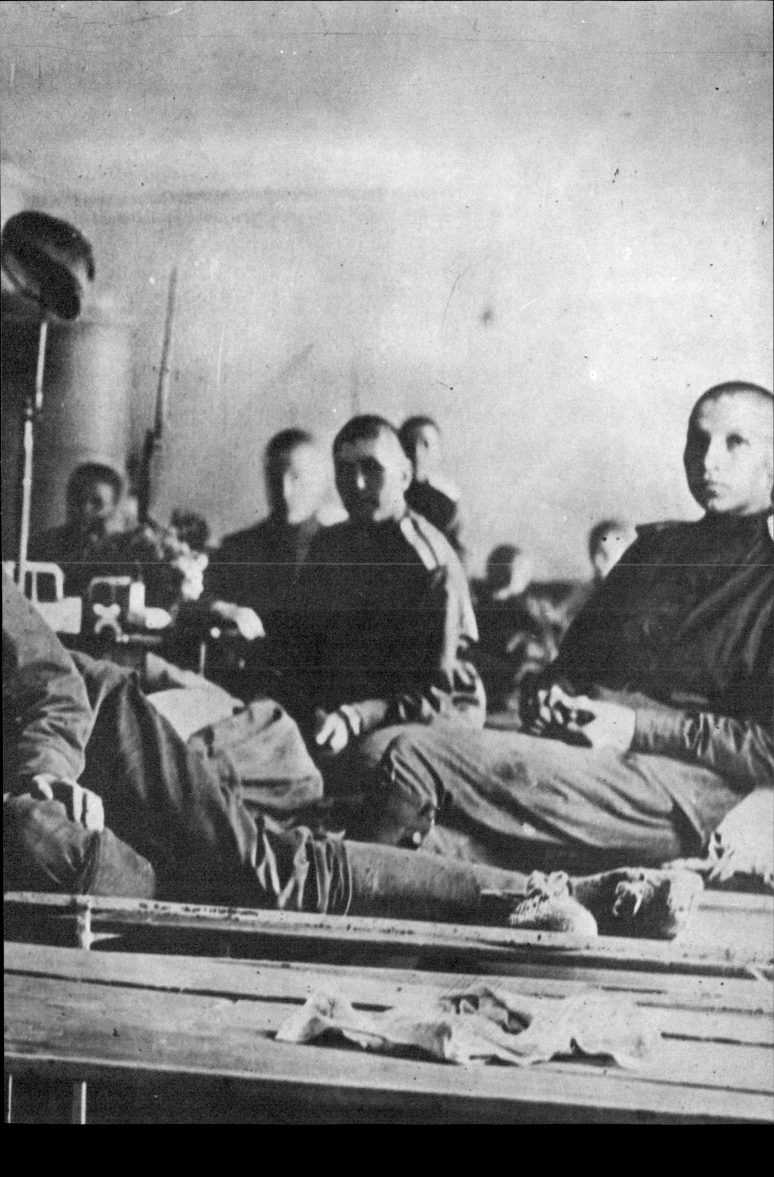

One of the principal early targets of the Revolution was the Russian Orthodox Church. Atheist parades were organized in the streets of large cities. Churches were pillaged and destroyed. Here Red Army soldiers remove icons and religious objects from a chapel.

on the Fortress of Peter and Paul hadn't been cleaned and oiled and were not fit to open fire. The Committee heard that the Winter Palace had surrendered. Two members went to verify the report, were fired upon and almost captured. The rumor, it was obvious, was not true. Finally, an ultimatum was delivered to the Winter Palace warning that an attack would be opened in half an hour (it was delivered by bicycle and had only five minutes to run when it was turned in). The Ministers refused to surrender and nothing happened. No attack was launched. But a panicking Government General surrendered the General Staff building to the Bolsheviks because he got tired of waiting on the telephone for an answer from the Malachite Chamber. Now the Provisional Government's writ ran only in the 2,000 rooms of the Winter Palace. It was obvious that the end was near.

At Smolny Lenin and Trotsky lay down on a blanket in a closet-like room to get a little rest. Lenin could not understand why the Winter Palace hadn't been assaulted. Trotsky offered to investigate but Lenin said he'd send someone to find out what was going on.

At about 10.30 the red lantern was run up and shrapnel shells were lobbed over the Neva river by the Fortress and blanks fired by the cruiser *Aurora*. Small guns and armored cars in the Square in front of the Palace opened fire. After half an hour the firing petered out and a telegraph agency reported the Bolshevik attack was weak and had easily been beaten off.

John Reed and Louise Bryant had been at Smolny waiting for something to happen. Now they hitched a ride on a truck and came to the Nevsky Prospekt, Petrograd's principal thoroughfare. The street was blacked out but they found a procession under way. It was made up of two hundred members of the City Duma which had voted to go to the Winter Palace and "die with the Government" if the Bolsheviks carried through their attack. The procession had been halted in the murk by a Bolshevik patrol of twenty Baltic sailors.

"Let us pass," a deputy shouted. "Let us sacrifice ourselves."

According to Louise Bryant a sailor retorted: "Go home and take poison but don't expect to die here. We have orders not to allow it." After an argument the delegates gave up trying to force their way through, went back to the City Duma and set up a "Committee to Save the Revolution".

At Smolny the Soviet began its session with an angry debate. Non-Bolsheviks attacked Lenin and his associates for trying to seize power and for shelling the Winter Palace. Lenin did not speak but Trotsky angrily responded that the opposition "are just so much refuse which will be swept into the garbage-heap of history".

At the Winter Palace members of the Military Revolutionary Committee busied themselves persuading cadets and other defenders to leave. About midnight they realized that the Provisional Government had only a handful of defenders left and a direct assault was ordered.

The first to notice the attack was the Palace switchboard operator. At 1.20 am she rang the phone in the Malachite Chamber and reported "a delegation of three hundred to four hundred is approaching". This was the assault force. Paintings, filmed enactments and heroic memoirs have painted the scene in vivid colors. Actually the throng of "attackers" simply crossed the Square and entered the auxiliary entrances to the palace. They swarmed up the broad staircases, (doing a good bit of looting on the way), and arrived at the Malachite Chamber just before 2 am. A small guard of armed junkers was prepared to defend Kerensky's ministers to the death but the ministers decided to surrender. At 2.10, a protocol of arrest having been signed, the Ministerial contingent was led out under the guard of Antonov-Ovseenko, a chief of the Military Revolutionary Committee, and taken to the Fortress of Peter and Paul. Casualties in the assault were six men killed.

It was 3.10 am October 27 when Lev Kamenev (one of the most sturdy opponents of Lenin's plans for insurrection) rose in the white-columned hall of Smolny Institute and announced officially the news which all had known for an hour or more — that the Winter Palace had fallen, Kerensky's ministers had been arrested and the Provisional Government was no more.

There was wild cheering but in a few moments the Soviet was plunged once more into a wrangle, this time touched off by peasant delegates violently objecting to the arrest and imprisonment of revolutionary members of the Kerensky Cabinet. The debate went on until 5.15 am. Lenin who had not made a public appearance all evening slipped away to a friend's apartment to work on the speech he was going to give on the evening of November 8 and to get a little rest.

The radical revolution to which Lenin had devoted his adult life had been achieved. How long it might last was the question now. Lenin himself was not too sanguine. He had never really believed that Russian radicalism could triumph on its own. It had to have the support and assistance of the revolutionaries of western Europe. His first objective would be to survive. If he and his Bolsheviks could stay on top for longer than the seventy-day life of the Paris Commune he would be pleased.

The cruiser Aurora *fired blank shells at the Winter Palace during the October uprising of the Bolsheviks.*

CHAPTER 13

For generations before 1917 the Russians had dreamed of true parliamentary government. All parties, Lenin's Bolsheviks included, had been committed before the October coup to support elections for a Constituent Assembly, that is, a freely elected Government. But Lenin began to have second thoughts when the November elections gave a huge majority to the opposition Socialist Revolutionaries. Posters appeared denouncing the Constituent Assembly. They claimed it was backed by French gold, the bourgeoisie and Czarist generals associated with Viktor Chernov, the head of the Socialist Revolutionary party.

FACING PAGE

The Bolshevik struggle for power was much more violent in Moscow than in Petrograd. Detachments of cadets and troops loyal to the Provisional Government barricaded themselves in the Kremlin and fighting went on for days. Finally the Bolsheviks won out with the aid of artillery which damaged many Kremlin buildings, including this Palace.

At 9 pm on the evening of the 26th, the hall at Smolny was once again jammed with soldiers in dirty greatcoats, peasants in sheepskins, workingmen in threadbare woollens and a sprinkling of white-collar intellectuals, as the Congress of Soviets convened for the second — and last — time. Lev Kamenev was in the chair. He called on Lenin, who in a businesslike manner began to present the Bolshevik program. Lenin wore a dark suit, somewhat rumpled, and hitched his thumbs into his waistcoat, occasionally emphasizing a point with his left hand. He was tired but exuberant.

He issued a call for immediate peace directed to all the warring nations, a just, democratic peace without indemnities or annexations. He asked for an immediate three-month armistice with Germany and expressed confidence that the working people of the world would hail the Russian initiative.

Everyone supported Lenin's proposal (all parties except the Left Socialist Revolutionaries had walked out of the Soviet the night before). They sang the "Internationale". They threw their caps in the air. They joined in a funeral dirge for comrades fallen in the struggle. Lenin led the singing from the platform. He had a good strong voice and he had always enjoyed singing. Some of the revolutionaries openly sobbed.

Then Lenin presented his decree on land. All private property rights in land were abolished — both for the big estate owner and the smallholder. All land became the property of the state. Only those who worked the land were to have the use of it — but the land of ordinary Cossacks and peasants would not be confiscated.

As Lenin conceded to the Assembly, this was in fact the Socialist Revolutionary land program. He had adopted it as his own. "Isn't it all the same who composed it?" he asked nonchalantly.

A Soviet of People's Commissars — all the members were Bolsheviks — was named to run the country and after more singing and debate (peasant delegates were still angry about the imprisonment of their leaders among the Kerensky Government in the Peter and Paul Fortress) the meeting dragged to an end at about 5.15 am.

Lenin had won. The Bolshevik coup had succeeded. The power, or most of it, was in his hands. But the crisis was just beginning. John Reed, the American witness of the October coup, reported that Lenin began his speech on that evening by saying: "We will now proceed to construct the Socialist order." This was, indeed, Lenin's task although good historical evidence indicates he never made that remark. Reed just got his notes mixed up.

How to construct the "Socialist order"? How to keep the power in Bolshevik hands?

The second question really came first. Even in Petrograd the Bolsheviks held on tenuously. Outside Petrograd no one knew what was going on. The Bolsheviks had staged an uprising in Moscow but it started very badly. Government troops and cadet detachments held the Kremlin and took the offensive against Lenin's supporters. Kerensky was rallying General Krasnov and his Cossack cavalry just outside Petrograd. They swept through Tsarskoye Selo and into Gatchina, last stop before Petrograd. The powerful Railway Workers Union informed the Bolsheviks it would not be a party to civil war. It would refuse to move anti-Bolshevik troops into Petrograd and it would not move Red troops outside the capital. On the weekend after the coup a handful of junkers staged a poorly planned counter-coup. It was easily smashed.

For a week it was touch and go. Then, gradually, the tide turned. Krasnov's Cossacks quit the battle and decided to go back to their Don country in the south. They almost succeeded in turning Kerensky over to the Bolsheviks but he escaped in a sailor's coat. Some of Lenin's supporters offered to remove both Lenin and Trotsky from the new government in return for backing by the railway union and the left-wing parties. Lenin's supporters split over his authoritarian tactics (he insisted on suppressing all but the Bolshevik press and instituting a censorship, just the kind of measures he had campaigned against when the Czar was in power).

Yet, somehow, shakily, Lenin managed to hold on. He got control of Moscow. Most of the big cities of Russia supported the new government but a great dilemma confronted Lenin, that of the Constituent Assembly. For a generation the election of a Constituent Assembly, a democratic parliament, had been the aspiration of every

Russian except extreme right-wing monarchists. From the moment of the February
Revolution all aims, all parties, had pointed to this election. Lenin, too, had pledged
the Bolsheviks to the Constituent Assembly, but now the elections had been held and
the Bolsheviks suffered a shattering defeat. True, they had carried the big cities of
Petrograd and Moscow by wide margins. But in the country as a whole the Socialist
Revolutionaries took 20,900,000 votes (58 percent); the Bolsheviks 9 million (25
percent), the Kadets and other bourgeois parties 4,600,000 (13 percent) and the
Mensheviks 1,700,000 (4 percent). Of the 704 seats in the Assembly the Socialist
Revolutionaries had 410 of which 370 went to the right-wing Socialist Revolutionaries,
the Bolsheviks 175, the Kadets 17, the Mensheviks 16 and the national minorities 86.

Youngsters enlisted in the early revolutionary days in a campaign against illiteracy. Each child carries a different letter of the Russian alphabet.

When the vote came in Lenin had his doubts. He was not going to turn his hard-won victory over to the Socialist Revolutionaries — or anyone else. What to do? Eventually, he adopted a simple solution. He let the Assembly meet. He appeared at the meeting with his Bolsheviks but quickly walked out. About 4 am one of the sailors on guard duty, Zheleznikov, came up to the Chairman, Socialist Revolutionary Viktor Chernov, and said: "It's time to quit. The guards are tired." The lights began to go off, the meeting dragged to an end and Russia's tiny experiment with constitutional democracy flickered out. When the delegates arrived at noon for the next meeting Lenin had posted guards at the Tauride Palace and had "prorogued" the session, just as the Czar used to "prorogue" the Duma. The Constituent Assembly never met again.

A greater problem was the war. A Russo-German armistice had been signed and at the fronts the Russians and German troops fraternized and played football matches against each other. Lenin sent Trotsky to Brest-Litovsk to take on the hard task of trying to negotiate a peace with the German military. But it was not so easy to negotiate Russia's release from the war. The year was 1918. World War I was in its last throes. The German High Command needed every possible resource to try for a knock-out blow on the Western front before the Americans arrived in decisive numbers. They were relentless in their demands for the grain of the Ukraine, the output of the Donets steel industry, the oil of Baku; and they knew Russia's armies were no longer capable of defending the country. Lenin kept hoping the Revolution would spread to Germany, to France, to England, but it did not.

Everything closed in on Lenin. The Germans had occupied most of the Baltic and the western reaches of the country — Belorussia and the approaches to Petrograd. Finland plunged into terrible civil war and was moving off on an independent course. So was Poland. An independence movement sprang up in the Ukraine and the Caucasus. In the south, generals hostile to the Bolsheviks had begun to build the foundations of the "White" Russian movement which would challenge Lenin's Reds.

Lenin was compelled to sign a devastating peace treaty with the Germans at Brest-Litovsk but even this gave him little respite. At any moment the Germans might attack again and Lenin had no forces with which to fight them.

The cities of Russia starved during the winter of 1917-18, none more painfully than Petrograd and Moscow. The police, battered by the February Revolution, had virtually disappeared after the October Revolution. Order fell apart. In January 1918 there were more than 15,000 burglaries of Petrograd apartments and houses, 9,300 holdups of shops and 135 murders.

Ariadna Tyrkova-Williams, a memorialist of the Revolution, one evening saw a crowd on the Liteniy Prospekt, one of Petrograd's principal streets. On a cart slowly jolting over the stone pavement, supported by the hands of women and soldiers, was a rag-like figure, head covered with a pot from which pitch dripped over the almost lifeless body. It was a "speculator" being subjected to lynch law by the crowd. The man had been hoarding *smetana,* sour cream.

Maxim Gorky encountered a crowd on the Fontanka, the stylish street leading off Nevsky Prospekt. They had caught three thieves — at least they thought they were thieves. They beat one, a youngster, to death. The other two they drowned in the Fontanka Canal.

One evening a band of sailors entered the principal hospital in Petrograd, killed two former ministers in Kerensky's cabinet who were being treated there, Shingarev and Kokoshkin, and made their escape. They were never found despite an urgent order from Lenin.

Two young Frenchmen were returning to France with their father, a teacher at a Petrograd school. They gave a small farewell party. Bolshevik Red Guards arrested the youngsters. In the morning the girls were released. The boys, all in their teens, three French and three Russian, were shot.

The newspaper *Nash Viekh* one morning published a plaintive commentary. There had been shooting the night before in Kirilovskaya Street and a witness saw five bodies carried out of the house at No 11 where a military unit was stationed. What had happened, asked the paper? Soviet authorities replied that five soldiers had been picked up drunk as they were preparing to rob a shop. They had been shot out of hand in the street. The newspaper complained that the answer wasn't satisfactory. It was true that five soldiers had been shot in the street. But the question had to do with five other persons, shot in an inner courtyard. This kind of occurrence became so frequent it almost ceased to cause comment.

The truth was that the fabric of Russian society was coming apart and Lenin could not hold it together. He took desperate steps. He began to arrest his political opponents. He set up a new organization which came to be notorious under the name of the Cheka — the Extraordinary Commission to Combat Counter-Revolution and Sabotage. At its head he placed Felix Dzerzhinsky, a Polish communist with a fanatical dedication to Lenin and the Revolution who was prepared to halt at nothing to preserve the cause of Bolshevism.

Now Lenin began more and more to invoke the doctrine of terror to strengthen his weakening grip. While he had opposed its use (in the form of assassination and terrorist attacks) as a revolutionary tactic Lenin had always emphasized that terror was a legitimate weapon in the struggle of a revolutionary regime to consolidate and hold power. As his wife Krupskaya recalled, he had often speculated that had the Paris Commune been prepared to employ terror against its enemies it might have survived. This was one mistake he did not propose to make, however much his associates might protest.

As trouble mounted, as complaints rose among workers and peasants, as more and more of Russia's political leadership appeared in the opposition, as the problems of feeding the country, enforcing law, holding any line against the Germans, the independent Ukrainians, the rapidly burgeoning Cossacks and military regimes in the South became more urgent, Lenin took draconian steps.

He sent military expeditions into the countryside to seize food from the peasants in order to feed the starving cities. Stalin headed one which went to Tsaritsyn, the old Volga city whose name ultimately was changed to Stalingrad and then, with Stalin's

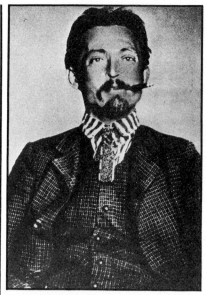

One of Lenin's first acts was to set up what came to be known as the Cheka — the Commission for Combatting Sabotage and Counter - Revolution—the forerunner of the modern Soviet Secret Police. He placed at its head a Pole, Felix Dzerzhinsky, a single-minded fanatic who came to be known as the "conscience" of the Revolution. In this early picture Dzerzhinsky looks more like a dandy.

This is a classic picture of Dzerzhinsky as Soviet propaganda portrayed the head of the Secret Police agency — an ascetic solely devoted to the defense of Lenin's cause.

In January 1918 Trotsky
went to Brest-Litovsk to
negotiate peace with the
Germans. He was
accompanied by A.A. Ioffe, a
Soviet diplomat who killed
himself in 1927.

OVERLEAF
Red Army parades in Red
Square. The Kremlin and
Spassky Bell tower in the
center, St Basil's cathedral to
the left.

Lord Rawlinson, commander
British expeditionary forces,
North Russia, interrogating
Bolshevik prisoner.

"unmasking", was rechristened Volgagrad. Hostages were swept up and held in prisons not only in Petrograd and Moscow but in every city and town of the country – to be shot if the enemies of the Bolsheviks executed or assassinated a prominent leader.

When Lenin signed his peace with the Germans at Brest-Litvosk he paid the price of giving up half the country and provoked a fearful row with his colleagues. Lenin now controlled a Russia no larger than the medieval Duchy of Moscow. He promised he would observe no more terms of his agreement with the Germans than he had to and moved Russia's capital "temporarily" from Petrograd to Moscow because Petrograd was too close to the German lines. After sixty years the capital is still in Moscow. A little more than twenty-five years ago Stalin shot a group of his principal associates whom he charged in the so-called "Leningrad affair" with plotting to move the capital back to Lenin's city.

It is hard to imagine a worse year than 1918 for the revolutionaries. The traditional army had been destroyed, in large measure through Bolshevik propaganda. The soldiers simply streamed away from the front. Now there were no reliable forces to face the Germans. There were no troops to oppose the hostile independent regime which had been set up in the Ukraine. Nothing to stand up to the White generals and their counter-revolutionary army in the South.

And even graver threats appeared. Scattered across the country through central Russia, the Volga, the Urals and out along the Trans-Siberian railroad were tens of thousands of former soldiers of the Austrian Empire, prisoners-of-war. These were Czechs who had surrendered to the Russians without fighting; at the outbreak of the Revolution they had been in transit, via Vladivostok, to fight the Germans in France.

The Czechs were an excellent fighting force, trained, disciplined and armed. The Bolsheviks tried to persuade them to join the Revolution. But they had little luck. The western allies, particularly the French, hoped to enlist the Czechs against the Bolsheviks.

The exact sequence of events is not entirely clear but midway into the spring of 1918

the Czech units began rising against local Bolshevik authorities in Siberia, taking over the Tran-Siberian railroad and the big Siberian cities. Their offensive quickly spread to the Urals, the Volga and other regions.

Red Army troops parade in Moscow's Red Square.

At the same time the Japanese landed troops at Vladivostok and the British, French and Americans prepared for armed intervention to bring Russia back into the war on their side (and incidentally to depose Lenin and his Bolsheviks).

To meet the emergency, Trotsky undertook to create a new "Red Army" out of the remnants of the Czarist forces and Bolshevik detachments raised among the city workers. He ranged the country in an armored train, garbed in a long-skirted military overcoat, leather gauntlets and peaked Russian cap with a five-pointed red star. He was seldom more than a day in any one spot because the threat was everywhere.

Conspiracy after conspiracy was launched against the Bolsheviks. Some came within a hair's breadth of success. Lenin's closest revolutionary collaborators, the left-wing Socialist Revolutionaries, became outraged at what they saw as the unprincipled "Maratism" of the Bolsheviks. Now they fell back on their old tradition of terror, but turned it against their erstwhile revolutionary associates.

Summer 1918 brought the violent Socialist Revolutionary campaign to a climax. Socialist Revolutionary terrorists assassinated the German Ambassador in Moscow, Count Mirbach. They shot the German commander in Kiev. They launched a coup, seizing the Cheka headquarters in Moscow, the post and telegraph offices and prominent Bolsheviks, including the Cheka chief, Felix Dzerzhinsky himself. Socialist Revolutionary military commanders took to the field, including the redoubtable adventurer Boris Savinkov who had directed some of the most spectacular Socialist Revolutionary assassinations. A handful of provincial centers were seized. The wave of terror was timed to coincide with the offensive of the Czech legions and the landing of French and British forces at north Russian ports, Murmansk and Archangel. The Socialist Revolutionary coup was easily crushed by Lenin but it left an aftermath of hatred, fear and suspicion.

Trotsky and his staff inspect troops in Red Square, Moscow. At his right, Antonov-Ovsenko, Trotsky's Political Commissar. On his extreme right, General N. Muralov, commandant of Moscow.

CHAPTER 14

This is the text of the official announcement of the execution of Czar Nicholas II in Ekaterinburg, dated 20 July, 1918.

ЭКСТРЕННЫЙ ВЫПУСК

По распоряжению Областого
Исполнительного Комитета Советов
Рабочих, Крестьянских и Солдатских
Депутатов Урала и Рев. Штаба бывший

Царь и Самодержавец
Николай Романов

расстрелян ~~~~~~~~~~
17 июля 1918 года.

~~~~~~ преданы погребению

Председатель Исполкома
Белобородов

г. Екатеринбург, 20 - июля 1918 г.
10   асов утра

Экстренный выпускъ отъ 20 iюля 1918 года
съ сообщенiемъ о разстрѣлѣ Царской Семьи

In the spring of 1918 the Romanov family was removed from its quiet and relatively comfortable exile at Tobolsk in western Siberia and taken to Ekaterinburg, capital of the Urals. Behind a wooden fence hastily erected around this house belonging to an engineer named Ipatyev the family was imprisoned until, on the night of July 16-17, all were shot.

I
n these critical days the melodrama of the Romanovs came to its inevitable climax. The Imperial family — the Czar, the Czarina, the four daughters and the Czarevich Alexis — had been living quietly in remote and non-revolutionary Tobolsk. Lenin's close associate, Yakov Sverdlov, was in direct charge of the Romanov problem. The Bolsheviks became increasingly hesitant to leave the family in Tobolsk because Bolshevik authority there was virtually non-existent and they feared a resolute and bold plan for rescuing the Imperial family might be carried out.

At the same time a radical Bolshevik group in Ekaterinburg in the Urals was violently agitating to get the family sent to Ekaterinburg. Sverdlov and Lenin seem to have been hesitant to send the Romanovs to Ekaterinburg because of fear that the left-wing Bolsheviks and left-wing Socialist Revolutionaries might simply execute them out of hand.

However, with some reluctance the Romanovs were finally transferred to Ekaterinburg in April and May of 1918.

It is probable that Lenin was preparing Ekaterinburg as a possible Bolshevik refuge if the enemy compelled him to give up Petrograd and Moscow. Several Soviet institutions had been sent there. Other members of the Imperial family were held in Perm and Alapayevsk, not far from Ekaterinburg. The Bolsheviks had planned to secrete the Russian gold reserve in the Urals, too, but it was captured by the Whites en route.

However, contrary to Lenin's expectations, the Urals quickly became the most threatened part of Russia. By July Czech forces were well on their way to taking over the whole Urals and the fall of Ekaterinburg quickly became a virtual certainty.

Since the February Revolution the question of a trial of the Czar, the Czarina and members of the Court camarilla had been debated. The Provisional Government conducted a lengthy inquiry into the regime of Nicholas II, examining the key officials of state and police as well as friends and associates of the Czarina. Kerensky personally questioned the Czar and Czarina rather cursorily, but the question of a trial was still open at the time of the Bolshevik coup.

It had always been assumed by the Bolsheviks that the Czar would be put on trial (and inevitably convicted and executed), but the unending crises pushed this project to one side. It was only because of the nagging of the Ekaterinburg Bolsheviks and growing reports and rumors of a plot to liberate the Imperial family from Tobolsk and whisk them out of Russia that orders were finally given to take the Romanovs to Ekaterinburg.

Events now rushed forward at a pace which dictated its own terrible solution.

FACING PAGE
The Czar and his family taking the sun on the roof of an outbuilding at their place of detention in Tobolsk, Siberia.

Judging from surviving evidence, the atmosphere in Ekaterinburg grew more and more tense. The Imperial family was confined in a big merchant's house in the center of town, owned by a family named Ipatyev. A wooden fence protected it from the street and a troop of surly Red Guards kept watch over the Romanovs and their small entourage (only four at the end – a doctor, a cook, a valet and a maid).

The Czar was a faithful diarist and his diary reveals that the family in late June and early July had some hope, however flimsy, of rescue. But that hope seems to have vanished in the first week of July and for the first time in his life the Czar halted his daily diary entries.

Meantime, the guard was strengthened. Letts and other non-Russians were brought in from outside. A tough Cheka officer named Yurovsky was put at its head and frantic consultations went on between the Ekaterinburg Communists and the Kremlin. Sverdlov, Lenin's chief aide, participated and so did Lenin although only a few traces of his personal intervention have come to the surface.

In early July a "show" trial of the Czar was actively considered in Moscow. Trotsky had asked Lenin for the privilege of appearing as prosecutor. An effort got underway to round up possible witnesses. The Ekaterinburg Bolshevik chief came to Moscow and stayed for a couple of weeks at the Kremlin, returning to Ekaterinburg only on July 12.

Meanwhile the Czech forces advanced relentlessly. On July 14 the Soviet military commander in the Urals warned that Ekaterinburg might be held for no more than three days. Just a month earlier the Bolsheviks had disposed of their first Romanov victim – the Grand Duke Michael in whose favor the Czar had abdicated. Michael, the most liberal of the Romanovs, had repeatedly made clear to the Bolsheviks that he had no desire to challenge the new regime. He was living under light surveillance in a hotel in Perm, not far from Ekaterinburg. One evening other guests at the hotel saw a half dozen men surround Michael and his English secretary, Johnson. After an altercation the pair were led out of the hotel and the next day the Bolshevik press claimed they had been spirited away by White Guardists. Actually they had been taken out of town and murdered by the Bolshevik Cheka.

Archbishop Germogen of Tobolsk had been very close to the Imperial family; he, too, was murdered about this time, once again by a Bolshevik convoy that was supposed to be escorting him. He was thrown into the Tura river and drowned near Pokrovskoye, Rasputin's birthplace.

On July 4 a very strict regime was installed at both Ipatyev House and at Alapayevsk where the Czarina's sister, the Grand Duchess Yelizaveta, the Grand Duke Sergei Mikhailovich and four Princes, sons of various Grand Dukes, had been held under very light supervision.

Ordinarily the Czar and his family spent an hour or so every day outside Ipatyev House, walking about the courtyard, taking the air. On July 16 this routine was broken. No one walked outside. At about 10 o'clock the family retired as usual. Some time after midnight, on the 17th, Yurovsky, the commandant, awakened them. He said the situation in Ekaterinburg was alarming and that they must rise, dress and come to the lower floor for safety. There had been alarms of this kind before and Yurovsky's news did not unduly upset the Czar and Czarina. They rose, washed, dressed and went down to a basement room at the back of the house. Three chairs were brought, one for the Czarina, one for the Czar and one for Alexis. The housemaid, Anna Demidova, brought along two pillows. Anastasia carried her sister Tatiana's little Japanese dog. There was a brief wait. Then Yurovsky, accompanied by eleven Chekists, burst into the room. He hurriedly declared that by decision of the Urals district committee the Czar and his family was to be shot. The Chekists instantly opened fire, each having been allotted a target in advance. Alexis did not die immediately and Yurovsky fired two more shots into his body. The corpses were carted off to an abandoned mine called the Four Brothers, chopped up, burned, drenched with acid and the ashes scattered so effectively that only odd bits of bone were ever found.

Late on the evening of the 17th word was received in Moscow that the executions had been carried out. An official communiqué was issued in Moscow on the 19th, reporting the execution of the Czar. It falsely said that the remainder of the family "had been taken to a safe place".

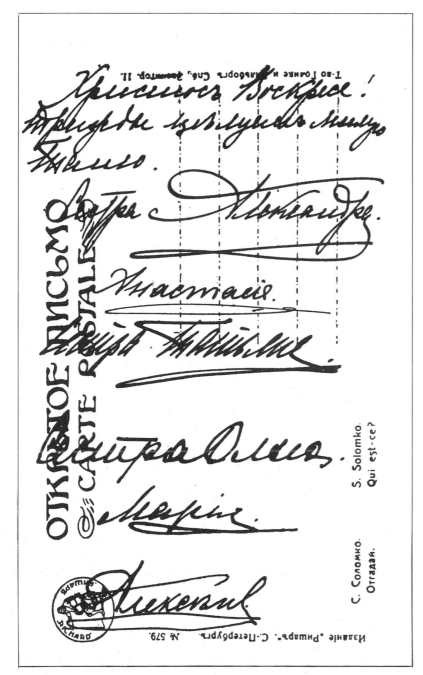

The same day on which the Czar's family died at Ekaterinburg the Romanov prisoners at Alpayevsk were murdered in the same manner and a false statement was issued that they had been killed by "unknown murderers".

Lenin's deliberately deceptive tactics, followed in each of the murders of the Romanovs, gave rise —as was intended — to all manner of rumor about the fate of the Imperial family. The Dowager Empress, mother of Nicholas II, went to her grave in 1927 convinced that her son was still alive. Legends about the survival of the Grand Duke Michael were persistent and for many years the Bolsheviks routinely denied all knowledge of his death. They were very sensitive to the fact that Michael's English secretary had been killed, apparently fearing English intervention. It was several years before the death of the whole Imperial family was officially acknowledged and the first official details were not released until 1921. Even so legends flourished that one or another member of the family survived the executions in Ekaterinburg. A favorite subject for speculation was the Grand Duchess Anastasia and for a generation or two "Anastasias" made their appearance at various spots, not unlike the false Dauphins who flourished in the early nineteenth century and were immortalized by Mark Twain in *Huckleberry Finn*.

CHAPTER 15

Kasimir Malevich,
Suprematism, *a 1920 gouache.*

No artistic movement of the Revolution was stronger than Constructivism in which Mayakovsky, Rodchenko, Lissitsky and many others played a role. It swept the field in typographical composition. Here is a page in a book for children How People Travel *designed by Olga Chichagova.*

Revolution! To the artists and poets, the painters and critics, the composers and playrights, this was the water in which they swam. As Tatlin put it, 1917 merely celebrated in the social field what art had already achieved even before the outbreak of World War I in 1914.

On the eve of the February 1917 Revolution artists, composers, writers and actors staged a great Carnival of the Arts in Petrograd. They hired (and painted) buses of every color and slowly paraded down the Nevsky Prospekt. Last in the procession was a truck on which had been splashed the words: Chairman of the World. On a chair, huddled in a soldier's greatcoat sat the radical poet Viktor Khlebnikov. The message was clear: the peasant soldiers were about to inherit the earth.

Now the poets walked into the Revolution as though it was a bus they had been awaiting for years. Or, as Viktor Shkolovsky, the Russian critic and friend of the poet Vladimir Mayakovsky, said: "Mayakovsky entered the Revolution as he would his own home. He went right in and began opening windows." Mayakovsky expressed his reaction to the Bolshevik coup in these words: "To accept or not to accept? There was no such problem for me (and other Moscow futurists). It was my revolution. I went to Smolny. I did everything that was necessary. Meetings began."

Mayakovsky was not exaggerating. It *was* his revolution, the one he and his fellow artists had dreamt, the one of which they had painted a prevision. Or so they thought. Cubism and Futurism, Malevich felt, were the advance forms of the Revolution. And now the task was to seize the world and build a new utopia for man.

There were, of course, the wildest kind of conflicts. Nothing had been more explosive than Russia's creative scene before October 1917. Now controversy widened. Mayakovsky took his place unequivocally beside the Bolsheviks. So did Andrei Bely, the mystic and visionary who spent the war with Rudolf Steiner and his anthroposophist cult at Dornach in Switzerland. And so, quintessentially, did Alexander Blok.

Blok came late to the Bolshevik coup. He had spent much of 1917 writing the history of the fall of the Czarist regime. Now he struggled with the images, those of Christ and of the grey-coated masses of peasant soldiery who had made the Revolution. He fell, as his diary reveals, into a frenzy out of which emerged the great poetic icon of the Revolution – his poem "The Twelve". It was published in March, 1918 and from that moment Russia could not escape knowledge of the true meaning of the Revolution.

Blok's vision was a terrifying one born in the ancient Russian beliefs of purification through sin, through blood, through fire. Twelve Red Guards march through the starving streets of Petrograd, casually turning their rifles at any target. In a gesture of

ТРУ-
13
БОКЪ

V. Lebedev, design for a ROSTA window poster.

The celebration of May Day, the traditional workers holiday, had been banned in Russia under the Czar. Now it became one of the great holidays of the year.

Kasimir Malevich in the most Russian of milieus — a country dacha set among pines and birches, wearing a rough peasant blouse. He is pictured four years before his death in 1935. He had painted little since 1928. He was buried in a coffin decorated with Supremacist designs.

Kasimir Malevich with Nikolai Suetin and Ilya Chachnik at Inkut, the Institute of Culture in Leningrad in 1923, one of the most controversial of revolutionary artistic groups, Suetin and Chachnik produced porcelain with Supremacist designs.

thoughtless violence one kills the prostitute whom he has once possessed and truly loves. The guards indulge in random looting. The wind whips through the streets, snow falls. Revolutionary clichés fall from their lips: "Keep the revolutionary step," "Forward, forward, Working people," "Let the bourgeoisie take care." The tramp of their feet goes on. And ahead the image of Christ suddenly appears, leading them through the blizzard.

No other literary work of the Revolutionary period stirred such a storm. Ivan Bunin was outraged. He insisted that Blok was appealing to cheap emotions. Zinaida Gippius, Blok's close friend and a determined enemy of the Bolsheviks, ranted against "The Twelve", especially when she saw its lines: "We'll start fires everywhere — let the bourgeoisie take care" plastered on the walls as a revolutionary slogan. And his words, "Don't be a coward — fire a bullet into Holy Russia!" made her sick. No one had been closer to Blok and to Bely. Now she did not even want to speak to them. When, months later, she encountered Blok in a streetcar, a pale worn figure of himself and he offered her his hand, she took it but told him she did so "only as a person". They no longer had anything in common so far as social views were concerned.

There were others who reacted gingerly to "The Twelve", most notably the Bolsheviks. Lenin never spoke a word about it. Anatoly Lunacharsky, the Commissar of Enlightenment, proposed to write an article about the poem but it never appeared. Kamenev thought that Blok "eulogized" Christ. In fact the Bolshevik leaders saw, too clearly, in "The Twelve" the mirror of the Revolution which they had always feared — not a trim, doctrinal, well-managed, pre-figured Marxist Revolution but the elemental peasant passion of Russia: that most irresistible of human forces, one which once aroused no one could master or control.

Constructivism and Suprematism, Proletcult (the Organization for Proletarian Culture) and most of the passionately debated styles and philosophies which contended and ravaged each other in the crucible of the Russian Revolution had already sprung to life before the politicians of 1917 caught up with the artistic avant garde (Proletcult, impressively, dated back to 1906).

But in the swirling events of 1917 and the relentless march of 1918 the artists formed and reformed their ranks, struggling for supremacy in the swift currents of Revolution. None, as it would transpire, would survive the mechanical jaws of Bolshevism. Those who managed to navigate through the years of Lenin's leadership fell victim to the stereotype imposed on Russia by Stalin with vigilant paranoia, which reflected the bourgeois taste of the 1890's in the Caucasus.

But all this was in the future. In 1918 Russia was falling apart. The British and French troops threatened the Bolsheviks from the north and mauled them in the

Caucasus and Turkestan. The Japanese connived with White Russian adventurers to claim eastern Siberia while the Americans under General Graves maintained an uneasy watch. White Generals launched their battalions north from the Don and the Kuban, and Ukrainian hetmen slaughtered the Red Army sent against them.

None of this halted the artists. There was no limit to their enterprise. On the first anniversary of the Revolution, November 7, 1918, Nathan Altman who had returned to Petrograd from Paris on the eve of World War I as an ardent Futurist, transformed Palace Square, the Winter Palace, the General Staff Arch. Russia was wobbling on the verge of collapse, but Altman was alloted 50,000 feet of canvas to mount Futurist constructions on the Palace walls and the General Staff Arch. The Alexander column was turned into Futurist sculpture. Red Square in Moscow was transfigured in similar style.

Two years later the Futurists again took over Palace Square. A central stage was erected, backed by Futurist designs. Giant arc lights "requisitioned" from an electrical contractor threw the scene into grotesques. A battalion of Red Army troops and thousands of Leningrad proletarians played out the storming of the Winter Palace.

As the pressures of World War I bore down on Russia's artists Malevich engaged in complex experimentation in form, shape and space, culminating in the white-on-white series of 1917-18 in which he eliminated all color and confined himself to pure white with a faintly pencilled outline. It was the limit to which such experimentation could be carried.

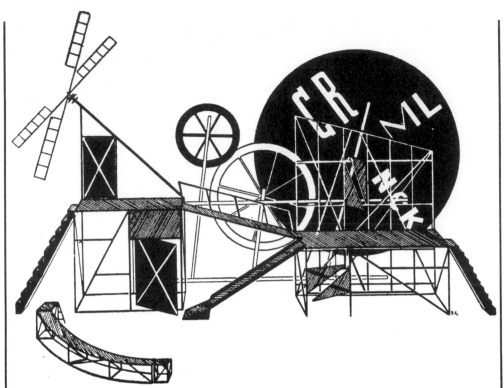

Fifty actors dressed as Kerensky made identical speeches and identical gestures on the stage. The Red Army and the proletarians remorselessly advanced, driving the anti-Revolutionary forces from the stage to the accompaniment of bells, horns, whistles, shouting.

It was a final flourish. What was called the era of "heroic Communism" was coming to an end. The commander of the Red Army battalion was reprimanded for letting his troops participate in a charade.

But for a few years Volga river steamboats were splashed with posters and slogans and sent down the great river, halting at every river town. Nadezhda Krupskaya rode on one. They carried Agit-Prop (Agitational-Propaganda) teams into remote parts of the country to lecture the peasants on the virtues of socialism. (While not many miles away detachments of armed Communists, sent out from Petrograd, were shooting down peasants who tried to protect their reserves of grain and cattle.)

The railroads burgeoned with agitational trains, painted like old-fashioned circuses except that the artists were Cubists and Futurists. Mayakovsky rode an agitational train decorated by Tatlin and conducted "symphonies" in which the instruments were factory steam whistles.

Nothing better epitomized the period than Vladimir Tatlin's construction – "Monument to the Third International". The Third International was Lenin's new international revolutionary movement, set up to replace the Second International which fell to pieces before the chauvinism of the socialist parties in World War I.

The monument was to be erected in the heart of Moscow and was, in a sense, to serve as a symbol of the new Revolutionary Russia and its world influence. The task was entrusted to Tatlin in 1919. He spent eighteen months constructing models and finally displayed his design "a union of purely artistic forms [painting, sculpture and architecture] for a utilitarian purpose" at the Eighth Congress of Soviets.

Utilitarian it was, but on an heroic scale, twice the height of the Empire State Building, a spiral fretwork reminiscent of the Eiffel Tower. Within the spiral was to be suspended a working building, a series of three revolving spheres. The first would revolve once a year, a higher one once a month and the top one once a day. The main sphere would be used for meetings and congresses; the second for offices and the top as an information center, transmitting by radio, telegraph, telephone and loudspeaker. There was to be a screen on which lighted bulletins would appear at night and a projector to cast images on low cloud formations where they might be read by the population of the whole city.

There was, of course, not a chance that this daring construct might be realized in steel and glass and concrete. Russia was not out of the Civil War period. What it needed was not flights of fancy, but bread, butter, shoes, work clothes and railroads.

Camilla Gray, the gifted historian of Russia's artistic explosion commented: "The tragedy of these artists lies in the contradiction between the Utopia that they envisaged and planned and conditions as they actually were. Most of their projects either remained on paper or were realized only in make-believe, in theatrical productions. But of such plans and ideas there was no shortage."

Some projects were simpler like Mayakovsky's window posters for ROSTA, the Russian Telegraph Agency. Every week he (and other artists) designed dramatic posters which were displayed by ROSTA in windows in Petrograd and Moscow and other Russian cities, caricatures of the young Revolution's enemies, appeals to patriotism or to class hatred, warnings against syphilis and appeals to brush your teeth.

Chagall's style incorporated strong elements of the Jewish Pale of Settlement from which he originated, as this painting of his 1912-14 period, The Rabbi, reveals.

RIGHT
Marc Chagall gives a painting lesson to orphans in the children's colony of Malakhovka set up after the Revolution not far from Moscow to care for children left without parents or home by the Revolution and civil war.

Chagall's native town in Russia was Vitebsk. In many of his paintings he reflected the life of the backward Russian towns of Belorussia.

FACING PAGE
There was an almost total symbiosis of Russian and French art in the years between 1905 and World War I. Many Russian artists like Marc Chagall worked in Paris but exhibited in Russia. Chagall stayed outside the avant garde cliques of Petrograd but contributed to the 1912 League of Youth show in Moscow. This painting, The Soldier Drunks, belongs to that period.

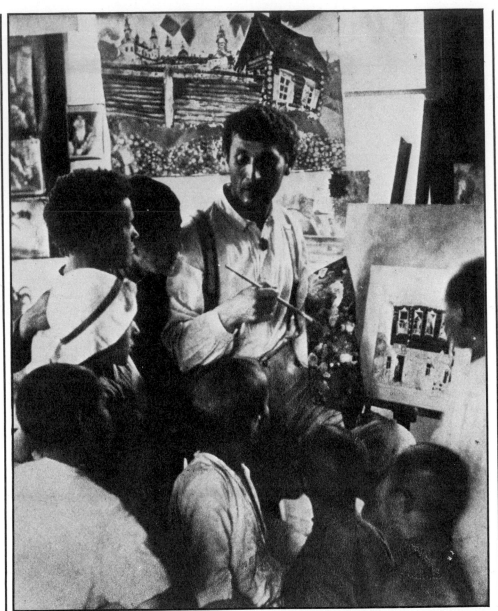

Alexander Archipenko, born
in 1887 in Kiev, was one of
the most influential sculptors
of the twentieth century.
Although he moved to Paris in
1908, and to the United States
(seen above aboard the SS
Mongolia with his bride of
two-years, German sculptress
Angelica Bruno-Schmitz) in
1923, he always thoroughly
influenced by his Russian
origins. As early as 1905 he
was expelled from art school
for criticizing his teachers for
being "too old-fashioned and
academic". Archipenko
became an American citizen in
1928. In 1937, he became
associate instructor at the New
Bauhaus School of Industrial
Arts in Chicago. He died in
New York City in 1964.

RIGHT
A 1920 bronze sculpture,
Geometric Figure with Space
and Concave.

FACING PAGE
Woman with Cat, 1910,
combines the economy of
abstract sculpture and the
earthiness of Russian folk art.

OVERLEAF
Rodchenko experimented in
many fields. This
photograph, which he took in
1927, shows the Red Army
on manoeuvers. The
illustration on page 201 was
done in the period following
his move to Moscow in
1915, when he launched
himself into the new and
radical technique of
abstraction and neo-
objectivism.

198

Left March! *was one of*
Maykovsky's most
revolutionary productions.
The book was designed by
Lisitsky.

FACING PAGE
A drawing from
Mayakovsky's revolutionary
poem: Left March!

OVERLEAF
Kandinsky; "Jaune, Rouge,
202 *Bleu," 1925.*

CHAPTER 16

This 1918 poster by D. Moor calls on Russians to volunteer to fight against the White Generals and the Allied Interventionist armies.

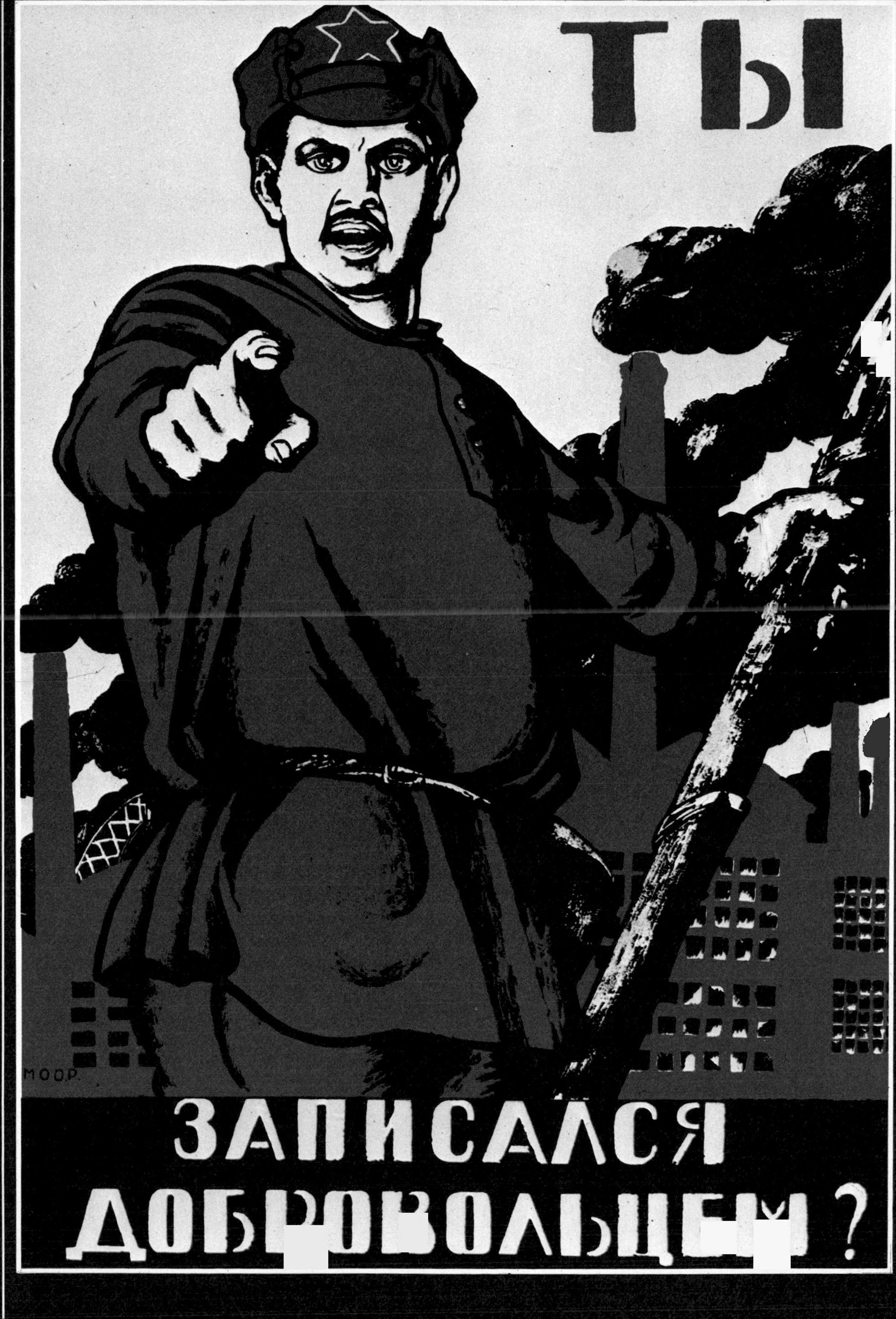
ТЫ
МООР.
ЗАПИСАЛСЯ
ДОБРОВОЛЬЦЕМ?

Maxim Gorky lent his name and prestige to Stalin's first great slave labor project, the construction of the Belomor, the White Sea Canal, connecting the White Sea with the Leningrad water navigation system.

The years 1918-19 passed for the Bolsheviks like a red blur. Lenin invented "War Communism" as a phrase to describe the struggle for survival. War Communism meant that anything needed for the Revolution was permissible. It was under this rubric that the Bolsheviks responded when, on August 30, 1918, Moses Uritsky, chief of the Petrograd Cheka, was assassinated by a young intellectual and, a few hours later, Lenin himself was seriously wounded by the dedicated Socialist Revolutionary Fanya Kaplan, who had been freed from prison by the Revolution, having served eleven years for an attempt on a Czarist official.

The call for terror sounded over Bolshevik Russia.

A Petrograd paper proclaimed: "Each drop of Lenin's blood must be paid for by the bourgeoisie and the Whites in hundreds of deaths. The interests of the Revolution demand the physical extermination of the bourgeoisie. They have no pity; it is time for us to be pitiless."

The Government ordered: "An end to this clemency and slackness! All Right Socialist Revolutionaries known to local Soviets are to be arrested immediately. From among the bourgeoisie and the officers, large numbers of hostages are to be seized. At the least sign of White Guard resistance or activity mass shootings are to be the rule without further discussion."

Action followed the words. The Petrograd Cheka shot 512 hostages, amongst them ten right-wing Socialist Revolutionaries. The victims included officers, industrialists, members of the aristocracy. Long lists of the names were published. Another 500 persons were shot at the Kronstadt fortress — all the prisoners who chanced to be in cells at the time. In Moscow there were sixty executions including those of several Grand Dukes and four former Imperial cabinet ministers. In Perm 86 lives were taken. In Penza 152, in Nizhni Novgorod 41, at Orlov 23, at Kursk 9. Hundreds of new hostages were arrested and warned they would be shot if further attempts were made on the lives of Bolshevik leaders.

One of the Cheka chiefs, Latsis, proclaimed a new doctrine. No longer was it necessary to investigate whether a person was guilty or innocent. A simple look at his hands and a question as to his parentage was all that was needed. If the hands were lily white and the parent bourgeois — he was guilty and could be shot without a qualm.

Pravda was not comfortable with the Latsis formula. It pointed out that Lenin would have been automatically executed under it. He came from a bourgeois background, his father a minor member of the nobility and he himself had the whitest of white hands.

Lenin seemed a little ambivalent. Gorky visited him in his convalescence. Gorky had thundered at the Bolsheviks in his newspaper *Novaya Zhizn* until it was finally suppressed by Lenin on July 16, 1918, the day of the execution of the Romanovs. In one of his last editorials Gorky directly challenged Lenin's theory of terror.

> Killing proves nothing, except that the killer is stupid. Punishment by death does not make people better than they are. However many people are put to death, those remaining alive nonetheless follow the path indicated by history — death is not strong enough to arrest the development of historical forces....
>
> Physical violence will always be an incontestable proof of moral impotence — this has long been known and it is time to understand it.
>
> To threaten a man with death for being what he is is illiterate and stupid.

Now emotionally overwhelmed by Lenin's narrow escape from death, Gorky visited his old friend (they had been linked in revolutionary aspirations since the beginning of the century and no one had raised so much money for the Bolsheviks in the days before November 7, 1917 as Gorky).

Lenin was recuperating near Moscow on the pleasant estate of the late Savva Morozov, the millionaire textile king who had poured hundreds of thousands of rubles into the Bolshevik cause, much of it passing through Gorky's hands.

The two old friends sat and talked in the autumn sunshine but there was no real meeting of minds. Lenin talked of the state of the country, of the "millions of peasants armed with rifles" of whom Gorky had written. He agreed with Gorky that this elemental force (the force which Blok had immortalized in "The Twelve") presented an anarchical threat to civilization itself. Only the Bolsheviks, he insisted, could cope with

this, only the Bolsheviks with their simplest of formulas, the Soviet and Communism. The intellectuals, Lenin contended, instead of firing bullets at him should be helping the Bolsheviks to handle this terrible threat. "They will be to blame if we break too many heads," Lenin told Gorky.

Lenin had another visitor that autumn. This was the remarkable and saintly revolutionary, Angelica Balabanoff. She had been in Stockholm and, alarmed by news of the attack on Lenin, hurriedly returned to Moscow. She was equally disturbed by the Party's public demands for the killing of hostages and the execution of Fanya Kaplan. She found Lenin in good spirits. He talked a great deal about the international scene and the mood of the workers. Finally she raised the question of the fate of Fanya Kaplan. Lenin seemed, she thought, ashamed of something. He said that the Central Committee must decide. Balabanoff thought he was pained by the idea that someone should be executed for trying to kill him. Later Nadezhda Krupskaya, Lenin's wife, threw her arms round Balabanoff and sobbed: "A revolutionary executed in a revolutionary country? Never!"

Regardless of these feelings Kaplan was, indeed, executed. A young Red Guard Officer named Pavel Malkov, commandant of the Kremlin and later a police official of some standing under Stalin, personally carried out the sentence. Kaplan, who was very near-sighted as a result of her long confinement in Czarist prisons, had been placed in a cellar room of the Kremlin. Malkov assembled a small squad of Latvian Chekists, removed Kaplan to the notorious Lubyanka prison by car and, at 4 am on September 3, 1918, killed her.

"And if," he wrote in his memoirs, "history repeats itself and again there appears before the barrel of my pistol a creature who has raised a hand against Ilyich my hand will not tremble when I cock my trigger as it did not tremble then..."

Malkov, obviously, was made of different stuff than Balabanoff, Krupskaya and — possibly, just possibly — Lenin.

Nowhere in Russia in that autumn of 1918 could Lenin discern a spark of hope. Bruce Lockhart, the British *chargé d'affaires* whose account of his activities in Russia reads like a novel by Ian Fleming, was deep in plots to bring down the Bolsheviks. He had an equally gifted associate, Sidney Reilly, a British agent who was eventually to be captured and shot on Soviet territory in 1928. Lockhart and Reilly had links to every force opposed to the Bolsheviks — monarchists, Kerenskyites, Socialist Revolutionaries, anarchists, ex-industrialists and soldiers of fortune — they had 1,200,000 rubles at their disposal, some of which went to disillusioned Red Army officers. Lockhart and some French undercover agents were arrested, the British Naval Attaché, Captain Cromie, was killed in a shoot-out at the British Consulate in Petrograd and Lockhart's plots were liquidated.

But there were other threats not so easily put down. Czech forces and anti-Red Russian troops had coalesced. They held Siberia, the Urals, most of the Volga and the Cossack territory. They were advancing north in the Volga valley, hoping to capture Nizhni Novgorod and push forward along the Kazan railroad toward Moscow.

The key to the operation was the little Volga town of Sviazhsk where Trotsky, the War Commissar, set up headquarters. To demonstrate to his comrades that he did not intend to abandon Sviazhsk under any circumstance, Trotsky had the locomotive uncoupled from his famous armored train and taken away.

To hold Sviazhsk was not easy. Against Trotsky were some of the most gifted opponents of the Bolsheviks, notably the famous Socialist Revolutionary terrorist and military adventurer, Boris Savinkov. Savinkov carried out a daring maneuver, encircling Sviazhsk from the rear and cutting communications with Moscow. An armored train tried to halt Savinkov but was captured and burnt. Trotsky's command began to disintegrate. The Political commissars fled, deserters commandeered a Volga river flotilla and cast off.

But Trotsky remained firm. He organized headquarters personnel, clerks, cooks and messenger boys. He had about 500 men left and they proved sufficient. He hurled back the attack, then, with fresh troops moved on Kazan. He executed thirty or forty deserters, and warned that anyone who had aided the Czechs and the Whites would be

FACING PAGE TOP
The bitter contention produced savage reprisals. Here are victims of an uprising hanged in Central Asia.

FACING PAGE BOTTOM
Trotsky proved himself the ablest organizer among the Bolsheviks. His oratory, his ability to keep constantly on the go, his skill in whipping the Red Army into shape saved the young Revolution from disaster again and again.

210

Peasants without food in the countryside made their way into the cities. This is Moscow's Arch of Triumph, erected to commemorate the victory over Napoleon in 1812.

Trotsky, War Commissar of the Bolshevik Government, exhorts Red Army troops from the tonneau of his open Packard touring car.

FACING PAGE
Trotsky was constantly on the go during the days of the Civil War with his peaked cloth helmet and its emblazoned red star, his heavy black boots, his massive greatcoat and his leather gauntlets. He stands beside his special train taken from the Petrograd-Moscow line.

Lenin confers with Trotsky.

OVERLEAF
Nadezhda Krupskaya, Lenin's widow, meets with a delegation of school teachers in Moscow in 1925. For the rest of her life she will devote herself largely to education.

214

shot. All bourgeois property would be seized and shared with the proletarians. By mid-September Trotsky had captured Kazan and Simbirsk, Lenin's birthplace.

The Bolsheviks stabilized their position on the Volga and soon a Socialist Revolutionary government which had been established at Samara would fall. But there were a score of other "governments" in the country – so many that a conference at the Urals center of Ufa was called in which the Samara Government, the Omsk Government (representing the Constituent Assembly which Lenin had prorogued), a half dozen Cossack regimes, councils for various Asian peoples, monarchists and others were represented. It was a salad that did not mix easily. Gradually more repressive military regimes took hold in Siberia. It was a time for rising White military figures, Denikin, Wrangel, Kolchak, Yudenich and many more.

To follow the crises, the battles won and lost, the shifting of alliances, the long slow, ponderous and, in the end, futile effort of the allied powers to turn the tide against the Bolsheviks is pointless. Enough to say that everywhere he looked Lenin saw disaster threatening – except when he looked to Germany.

World War I had entered its final weeks. In November, Germany collapsed. The armistice was signed and Lenin's great hope seemed to be coming true – the German revolution. The German fleet rose. Soviets were established in the cities. The red flag flew over Kiel. The Spartacus League, the German counterpart of Lenin's Bolsheviks, seemed on the road to power. Lenin was ecstatic. His wife Krupskaya recalled the early days of the German rising as "the happiest of [Lenin's] life". But it was a short-lived happiness. Power went to the more conservative Social Democrats. The revolutionary heroes, Karl Liebknecht and Rosa Luxemburg, were brutally murdered. Lenin's hopes for German revolution, for European revolution, died slowly. But they died.

Since childhood Christmas had been the great holiday of Lenin's life. The Ulyanov family had always celebrated a German Christmas, not a Russian Orthodox one, for Lenin's mother was of German descent, a Lutheran, not a Russian Orthodox. Now Revolution had come, and Lenin and his comrades had launched vicious attacks against organized religion, particularly the State-supported Russian orthodoxy. Crude campaigns against religious belief and in support of atheism were the ordinary currency of Party policy. But nothing disturbed Lenin's dedication to Christmas.

As the grim year of 1919 was getting underway Krupskaya was recuperating from illness at a children's school in Sokolniki, a forested park on the outskirts of Moscow. Lenin decided to give the children a Christmas party. He had missed the actual date of Christmas by the Orthodox calendar, so the party was given on Twelfth Night, January 19. He started out for Sokolniki in a car driven by his chauffeur, Stepan Gil, accompanied by his sister, Maria Ilyinichna, and his bodyguard, Cherbanov. As the car entered Sokoloniki six or seven men halted the machine. Lenin thought it was a military patrol. They ordered the party out of the car. Lenin showed his Kremlin pass and said: "My name is Lenin." They took the pass, and also a small Browning revolver he was carrying. His sister cried: "What are you doing – This is Comrade Lenin. Who are you? Where's your authority?"

One of them quietly replied: "Criminals don't need any authority."

The bandits jumped into Lenin's Packard and sped away – carting off the presents he had bought for the children.

To such an estate had Russia fallen.

CHAPTER 17

Into every corner of Russia the Bolsheviks carried their campaign against illiteracy. This poster equates illiteracy with blindness. Illiteracy leads peasants into failure and accident.

НЕГРАМОТНЫЙ тот-же СЛЕПОЙ
ВСЮДУ ЕГО ЖДУТ НЕУДАЧИ И НЕСЧАСТЬЯ·

What had Lenin's Soviet turned out to be? Well, it bore little resemblance to any model of socialism which had been dreamed of by Karl Marx, Frederick Engels or Vladimir Lenin. It operated in an arbitrary, often contradictory, manner. The peasants in most places had simply taken over the land in 1917 and 1918. They killed any landowners who remained in the countryside, burned down the large manor houses, granaries and outbuildings, slaughtered the cattle, horses, sheep and pigs and let the machinery go to ruin. By 1919 most of them were growing just enough food for themselves and simply trying to survive. Any military force, whatever its colors, which entered the countryside seized whatever foodstuffs it could find.

Lenin was eager to set up peasant cooperatives – the forerunners of collective farms – and state farms which were supposed to be exemplary enterprises which would teach the peasants modern, efficient farming methods. Not much was done on either score. The regime was too busy trying to survive.

If farming was in a state of chaos, industry and trade were even worse. Lenin had come to power with the notion that any clerk could run a bank. He quickly found this was not true. In fact he had difficulty even getting control of the banks and the money because the bankers declared a sitdown strike. (The same thing happened in many branches of the government. The bureaucrats either wouldn't give the Soviet officials the keys, or walked away and let the new bosses find out how to run the institutions on their own.)

All big factories, mines and other enterprises were nationalized within a few months. In some cases the workers tried to run them. In others the former owners were asked to keep them going. Neither alternative worked well. The workers weren't accustomed to managing large-scale operations. The former owners often sabotaged the business. With the breakdown in transportation and lack of resources even a genius had a hard time making anything work.

People streamed out of the cities. Moscow lost half its population, Petrograd almost two-thirds. External trade sank to zero. The allies imposed a total blockade. Nothing came into the country. Nothing went out. Railroad locomotives burned wood. The only commodity in ample supply was paper money; by the start of 1919 nearly 34,000 million rubles in paper notes were in circulation. A year later it was ten times worse. A pack of cigarettes cost a million rubles. Gunnysacks of paper rubles would not buy potatoes from the peasants in the field. Commandos swept down on black markets, confiscating food and goods and shooting "speculators". The markets opened for business in the same place the next day. No one could live without them.

In the cities water supplies failed and toilets did not work – cold froze the pipes. People huddled around *burzhuiki,* little tin stoves with a pipe out the window, fed by torn pages from books and broken legs of old chairs. Such conditions would not be seen again until World War II and Leningrad's 900-day calvary by seige. Cholera swept the country. Young people, men and women, shaved their heads to defeat the germ-carrying lice. Strikes spread through the factories, and even veteran Bolsheviks who had survived the Czar's police underground and in prison began to question Lenin's regime.

The ancient Imperial Czarism was dead. But a new socialist proletarian regime had not been born. When Lenin founded the Third International to carry the revolutionary word to the world it had thirty-five delegates, most of whom spoke only for themselves. France was represented by Jacques Sadoul, an attaché of the French military mission who had stayed on in Russia as a Bolshevik sympathizer. Boris Reinstein represented the United States. A Dutchman named Rutgers represented the Japanese. The only real foreign Party which took part was the German Spartacus League. Its representative refused to vote on the founding of the new International because he had not been authorized by his party. Lenin's spirits were so low that even this sham organization gave him a lift.

What *was* Lenin's dream of communism in practical terms? It is not an easy question to answer. Like Marx before him, Lenin was a glib and often discerning critic of the existing capitalist world but not imaginative in planning what was to succeed it. He believed that the exploitation of man by man should cease and that no one should profit by another's labor. He did not perceive that another alternative might arise

Pictures of Lenin and Trotsky are common in the period before Lenin's illness and death. Here Lenin speaks to a crowd in Theater Square with the Maly Theater at his back. Trotsky stands below Lenin at the right side of the rough wooden

220 *podium.*

The Bolsheviks employed every kind of propaganda medium to shore up their regime. Artists decorated propaganda trains which were sent across the country filled with orators and brass bands to rouse enthusiasm for the Revolution. Propaganda boats plied the rivers. Lenin sent his wife, Nadezhda Krupskaya, out with a propaganda boat on the Volga. The trains and boats were decorated by avant garde artists and poets wrote special verses not only praising the Soviet regime but urging peasants to brush their teeth, take precautions against venereal disease and learn to read and write.

This propaganda train decorated in a style reminiscent of Mayakovsky proclaims: "The bourgeois owners of the theaters poisoned the spirit and minds of the People. Now the theater belongs to the People."

FACING PAGE
Propaganda workers are offloading stacks of pamphlets from the propaganda train. The car is designated as the "Newspaper Window" and is decorated with newspaper headlines and slogans.

Lenin with leaders of the
Third International in the
Kremlin. Lenin is at head of
table. Midway down the
table on his left is Leon
Trotsky.

Youngsters like this were fed by the American Relief Administration in 1921.

which would devour the bodies and labor of men and women by the million — exploitation by the state, state capitalism or, as under Stalin, state slavery.

Lenin believed, or insisted that he believed, in the "withering away of the state", that is, gradual transition to a society in which state control and coercion no longer existed (Marx preached that the State was simply the organ of repression of the ruling class). No forecast of Lenin or Marx proved more elusive than the "withering away" of the state. Stalin finally abolished the theory, saying, in effect, that it could not come about until the whole world became Communist. Meantime, he proceeded to erect the world's greatest, most bureaucratic, dictatorial state.

Lenin believed in a moneyless economy, a society in which each would contribute according to his ability and be rewarded according to his need. Money would vanish, as well as money relationships.

Of course, nothing like this occurred. Money did disappear to an extent in 1920, simply because inflation made a money economy meaningless. But the new slogan was: "He who does not work, neither does he eat." The bourgeoisie was prohibited from normal occupations and compelled instead to clean streets and shovel snow. The children of the bourgeoisie were banned from higher education.

Sex equality was a plank in the Bolshevik platform. But Lenin was a prude and fought women colleagues like Alexandra Kollontai who spoke for a woman's right to choose her sexual partners as she pleased on the theory that love was "just a glass of water". Lenin did not believe in free love. Nonetheless one of the most effective propaganda claims against his regime was the contention that the Bolsheviks had "nationalized women".

There was one more thing. Lenin was a practical man. He could see as well as anyone that Communism had given Russia little but struggle, death, suffering and disease. What could be done to realize the utopian dreams on which his life and that of the revolutionary generation had been based?

Electricity! He fell into correspondence with one of his oldest Bolshevik associates, Gleb Krzhizhanovsky, chairman of Gelro, the State Electrification Authority. His friend told him about long distance transmission of electrical power in the United States, bringing electric light to the smallest farmhouse. Lenin was entranced. He called on Krzhizhanovsky to draft plans for creating a system capable of supporting 20,000,000 or even 40,000,000 light bulbs. Light should enter all rural district centers within a year; all villages in two years. Every village library was to get *two* light bulbs.

Finally Lenin had his definition. He proclaimed (in 1920): "Communism is Soviet power plus electrification of the whole country." An illuminated display on the stage of the Bolshoi theater twinkled with white and red lights showing the power plants that would be built and the villages that would get electric bulbs. Lenin had to send a personal note to the manager of the Bolshoi theater to get permission for the workmen to stay in the theater after closing hours to get the display done in time for the delivery of his report.

Gradually the military tide turned. Slowly at first. Then more rapidly. Trotsky had whipped the Red Army into shape. He took on the great enemies of the Revolution serially. It was up and down. But the peasants began to realize that ruthless as the Bolsheviks were, the Whites were even more ruthless. The Whites took not only the peasant's food but his life and his land. Throughout 1919 the balance swung. Denikin captured Kharkov. He swept up the Volga and retook Tsaritsyn. He was closing in on Moscow. Yudenich moved into the suburbs of Petrograd. Once again Lenin was thinking of fleeing to the Urals. But Trotsky routed Yudenich in the Petrograd suburbs. Then he turned on Denikin, whose army had begun to fall apart. Red troops swept after Admiral Kolchak in Siberia, driving him back from city to city toward the Far East and extinction. Baron Wrangel still held on grimly in the South but the allied interventionists were packing up and getting away, taking with them the remnants of White organizations around the Black Sea.

There was one more military chapter to be played out. As the Civil War drew toward a close, the Poles under General Pilsudski invaded the Ukraine and occupied Kiev. The battle-hardened Red Army set out to rout the Poles, led by its new heroes, Tukhachevsky and Yegorov, both of whom won their spurs in the Civil War. Stalin acted as Yegorov's political commissar. The Red Army was in high spirits and soon

had the Poles in full retreat. Lenin wanted them to push on to Warsaw, Trotsky was dubious of the adventure. Stalin, who hoped to fashion a military reputation to rival Trotsky's, persuaded Yegorov to head for Lvov instead of Warsaw. It was a disastrous move. Tukhachevsky advanced on Warsaw without Yegorov's support and was caught by shrewd Polish tactics devised by a French military mission. Peace was signed with the Poles and in mid-November Wrangel evacuated the Crimea.

The triumph Lenin had hoped for in Poland had turned into disaster, but the long war was over. Lenin sadly turned his sights inward to see what might be done for his poor, battered, starving, bankrupt country.

Lenin suffered one more blow, a personal blow. Inessa Armand, the beautiful French-Russian woman who had burst into the late years of his life like a red flame, died of cholera in the Caucasus on September 24, 1920 at the age of forty-one. She was one of the 12,054 cholera deaths reported to the Commissariat of Health up to September of that year.

It was a heavy blow. Balabanoff had never seen Lenin so shaken as at the funeral. "Small as he was," she recalled, "he seemed to shrink and grow smaller. He looked pitiful and broken in spirit. I never saw him look like that before."

Inessa's ashes were placed in the Kremlin wall.

Soon another urn found its place in the wall beside that of Inessa. It was that of John Reed, the American chronicler of the Revolution and friend of Lenin's. The revolutionary circle was beginning to grow smaller.

Almost none of the great designs and architectural plans of the revolutionary artists could be carried out. There were no funds for grandiose buildings. The best that most could do was to create models or sometimes scenery for avant garde theatrical productions.

Vladimir Tatlin, one of the most imaginative of the Constructivists, created a monument to the new Third International which had just been founded by Lenin. The structure was supposed to be twice the height of the Empire State building. Within a steel spiral was to be suspended a glass cylinder, a glass cone and a glass cube. Each would revolve — the cylinder once a year, the cone once a month, the cube — on top — once a day. The cylinder would house meeting halls; the cone offices; the cube an information center which would broadcast by radio, telephone, telegraph and loudspeaker. Messages would be flashed to the heavens and reflected down on Moscow by cloudy skies.

230

CHAPTER 18

The Intervention was over —
but not Soviet hatred for the
big capitalist states. This
caricature is called: The
League of Nations. France,
the USA and Britain sit
together under the banner
"Capitalists of All Nations
Unite!"

ЛИГА НАЦИЙ

Пролетарии всех стран, соединяйтесь!   „Желтый Интернационал".   Российская Социалистическая Федеративная Советская Республика.

n February 26, 1921 the battleships *Petropavlovsk* and *Sevastopol* lay frozen in Kronstadt harbor. These were famous ships, the *Petropavlovsk* had played a role in the October Revolution and the *Sevastopol* was known as a stormy, revolutionary ship. On that day an icy wind blew off the Gulf of Finland and the temperature dropped close to zero. The crews of the two vessels met and voted to send a delegation to Petrograd to investigate what was happening. They had heard rumors that red Petrograd was on strike, factories had been closed down, government troops were firing on demonstrating workers and executing strikers by the dozen in the cellars of the Cheka headquarters at No. 2 Gorokhovskaya, once the Czar's Prefecture.

The angry sailors made their way into Petrograd. They found armed troops and Communist cadets surrounding the factories; streets filled with indignant people; shops closed for lack of food. Workers had been arrested by the hundred. Many of them were locked out of their plants. Theaters stood dark, restaurants shut, a curfew had been imposed.

Petrograd (and all the cities of Russia) had been starving for months. Then, in late January, the Government had again cut the bread ration (800 grams a day for heavy industry; 600 grams for shock workers and 400 for ordinary workers) by one-third. Wages had dropped to less than one-tenth pre-war levels. Petrograd's population was possibly 500,000, compared with 2,500,000 in 1914.

Roadblocks had been set up at every entrance of the city. Workers who went to the country to gather food were halted at these barriers. Often their food was confiscated, many times they were arrested or shot. In the factories military discipline was installed, and military rules of punishment. The Taylor system, an American method of labor measurement and control by which Lenin was fascinated, was being introduced (in the United States militant trade unions fought successfully against it, claiming it turned the worker into a robot).

In January 1919, two remarkable figures had reached Russia, Alexander Berkman and Emma Goldman, both American anarchists of Russian birth. Together with 247 other American radicals they had been deported from the United States aboard the old Army transport *Buford*.

Now, in February 1921, Berkman was in Petrograd, watching events with rising apprehension.

> At dusk, [he noted in his diary] old women prowl about the big woodpile near the Hotel Astoria, but the sentry is vigilant...Crowds of strikers gathered in the street near the mills and soldiers were sent to disperse them...nervous feeling in the city...Martial law....
>
> At the Soviet session last evening a military member of the Defense Committee denounced the strikers as traitors to the Revolution. It was Lashevich. He looked fat, greasy and offensively sensuous. He called the dissatisfied workers 'leeches attempting extortion'...

Rumors spread of outbreaks in Moscow. The rumors were true. Factory workers had even jeered at Lenin and demanded that he clear out. Demonstrators appeared in the streets. Some carried banners calling for the Constituent Assembly – that long vanished dream of Russian democracy. Others bore anti-Semitic slogans: "Down with Communist Jews." (Many peasants thought there was a difference between a Bolshevik and a Communist. They supported the Bolsheviks whom they thought had let them take the land and opposed the Communists whom they believed robbed them of their grain and foodstuffs.)

In Petrograd the strikes spread from factory to factory – the Trubochny, the Laferme tobacco plant, the Skorokhod factory, the Baltic and Patronny metal works, the Admiralty shipyards, the Putilov plant.

Socialist Revolutionary and Menshevik agitators – those who had not yet been wiped out by the Bolshevik terror – reappeared in the streets. Leaflets demanded the release of political prisoners, an end to martial law, free speech and civil rights. Zinoviev, Party boss of Petrograd, became alarmed. He telegraphed Moscow for troops, fearing that the Petrograd garrison sympathized with the local unrest.

Not a few persons noted the fateful coincidence in time. Precisely four years earlier,

Emma Goldman, the American anarchist, was deported in 1921 in the post-World War I anti-red hysteria. She and her fellow anarchist, Alexander Berkman, were sent to the Soviet Union where they quickly became disillusioned. She is second from the left. Center is Alexandra Kollontai, strong supporter of Lenin, feminist, who once said that for a woman, love should be no more important

234 *than a glass of water.*

El Lissitsky designed this poster on Constructivist principles to rally the Bolshevik forces in the Civil War. It is called "Beat the Whites with the Red Wedge". It is dated Vitebsk, 1919.

ABOVE AND OPPOSITE
Lenin spoke at the dedication of this monument to Karl Marx and Frederick Engels in the square in front of the Bolshoi Theater in 1919. Later Stalin took down the statue and covered the square with asphalt so he could more easily move troops and tanks to defend the Kremlin — in case of need.

in the same week at the end of February and the beginning of March, disorders began in the streets of Petrograd which brought the Czar's regime crashing down. Would history repeat itself? Would Lenin and the Bolsheviks suffer the same fate?

Berkman's diary told the story day by day. The sailors of the *Petropavlovsk* and the *Sevastopol* reported to their comrades at Kronstadt. They demanded the election of new Soviets by secret ballot, freedom of agitation, freedom of speech for all peasants, anarchists and left-wing parties, freedom of assembly for trade unions and peasant organizations, the liberation of political prisoners, inquiry into the cases of all being held in prison and concentration camps, abolition of all political departments and commissars, removal of roadblock detachments, equalization of rations, abolition of Communist detachments in the army and Communist guards in factories and mills, and freedom for peasants to keep their land and cattle.

What the sailors asked for was a return to October 1917, when Lenin had come to the top with the slogan "All Power to the Soviets". What they wanted was a return to Soviets freely elected — an end to Lenin's hard-won, elitist principle of a tight Bolshevik monopoly.

There wasn't a chance that Lenin would agree.

Berkman attended a meeting at the Tauride Palace which was packed with Communists, mostly youngsters. Factory delegates attempted to state their case. They were shouted down. Zinoviev called the strikers "enemies of the Soviet regime". Mikhail Kalinin, the Soviet President, charged that Kronstadt was the headquarters of a White Guard conspiracy. A resolution demanded immediate surrender.

"It is a declaration of war," Berkman noted. He was right. Trotsky came to Petrograd and issued an ultimatum: Immediate submission or he would "quell the mutiny and subdue the mutineers by force of arms".

"The city is on the verge of panic," Berkman recorded. "The factories are closed. Threats against the Jews are becoming audible. Trotsky has sent another demand to Kronstadt containing the threat: "I'll shoot you like pheasants."

Berkman could not stand by idly. He and Emma Goldman appealed to Zinoviev to be permitted to mediate. Berkman said: "Comrades Bolsheviki, bethink yourselves before it is too late! Do not play with fire; you are about to take a most serious and decisive step!"

It was of no avail. On March 7 he jotted in his diary: "Distant rumbling reaches my ears as I cross the Nevsky. It sounds again, stronger and nearer, as if rolling toward me. All at once I realize that artillery is being fired. It is 6 pm. Kronstadt has been attacked! My heart is numb with despair. Something has died within me."

Something died, and not only within Berkman. Ten days later Kronstadt fell. The sailors, the most radical supporters of the Revolution, the hardcore on whom Lenin had relied even when he could not trust his own comrades in the Bolshevik Central Committee to support the idea of the October uprising, had been crushed in blood and agony. About 8,000 defenders of Kronstadt made their way over the ice to Finland. Some 600 died in the fighting, not a few were massacred in the final Red Army assault. More than 1,000 were wounded and 2,500 taken prisoner. Of the prisoners, thirteen were tried and executed as ringleaders. Several hundred were shot almost immediately and, of those remaining, several hundred more were shot in the ensuing months; the remainder were sent to the dread Solovki prison on a White Sea island, once a monastery. Soviet casualties were far higher — repeated assaults over the ice took a frightful toll. The total killed, wounded and missing, has been estimated at 10,000.

The cost in lives was tragic. The cost in spirit was greater. Berkman wandered the bleak streets of Petrograd in despair. Goldman sat in the Astoria Hotel unable to stir. To her Petrograd seemed a "ghastly corpse". The next day when she heard the bands playing the "Internationale" in celebration of the fiftieth anniversary of the Paris Commune, "its strains once jubilant to my ears now sounded like a funeral dirge for humanity's hope."

In that moment Berkman and Goldman determined to leave Russia. Before the year was out they had abandoned the Soviet Union and their bright hopes. Emma Goldman was to write:

Violence, the tragic inevitability of revolutionary upheavals became an

established custom, a habit and was presently enthroned as the most powerful and "ideal" institution. Did not Zinoviev himself canonize Dzerzhinsky, the head of the bloody Cheka as the 'saint of the Revolution'? Were not the greatest public honors paid by the State to Uritsky, the founder and sadistic chief of the Petrograd Cheka?

This perversion of the ethical values soon crystalized into the all-dominating slogan of the Communist Party: THE END JUSTIFIED ALL MEANS.

Lenin knew the meaning of Kronstadt. Nearly a month earlier he had written to an associate: "We are beggars. Hungry, ruined beggars."

It was true, economically, politically, spiritually. Lenin had had his way. He had beaten all the others. Of the Czar's Empire he now ruled the greater part. Poland, Finland and the Baltic States had split off, but of the rest he was master, barring the remains of independent entities in the Caucasus – and these were being attended to.

But he had inherited a corpse. Of Marxist dreams and revolutionary ideals – hardly anything remained. And still the struggle to maintain power had not ended. He had been willing, in March of 1918, to give up half of Russia in order to ensure the survival of Bolshevism in the remnant. Now he gave up Marxism itself in order to stay in power.

Lenin went before the Tenth Party Congress in mid-March. The cannon of Kronstadt still echoed across the frozen ice. He won the approval of what the Marxist D. B. Riazanov called a new Brest-Litovsk – this time it was a treaty with the peasants. It came to be known as NEP – the New Economic Policy. What it meant, in effect, was that Lenin had abandoned War Communism and the arbitrary seizure of food from the peasants. Now he introduced a tax-in-kind and freedom for the peasant to sell his food in the market. Armed roadblocks were abandoned. Trade between city and countryside was encouraged. Labor armies (Trotsky's invention) were abandoned. Private retail shops were welcomed back. Private entrepreneurs were invited to resume production of consumer goods. The private theater returned. So did private publishing. Foreign capitalists were lured to Russia with offers of concessions; in return for bringing their capital and know-how they were given contracts to operate mines and factories for fixed-price leases over a period of years, the capitalists and the Soviet sharing the profits. Foreign trade was encouraged, diplomatic relations began to be normalized and there was a sharp reduction of revolutionary rhetoric directed into international channels.

But there was no increase in internal political freedom. Mensheviks, anarchists and surviving Socialist Revolutionaries were rounded up by the thousands and imprisoned or sent to Siberia. Their activities were banned. Lenin imposed new Party rules which forbade factional quarrels. The "Workers Opposition" was suppressed. The Central Committee won secret powers to expel any dissident and a quarter of the Party had been purged before 1921 was out.

Once again by draconian measures Lenin stayed in power. Angelica Balabanoff found a famous confectionery store next to the National Hotel in Moscow where she lived suddenly reopened with every kind of candy, pastry, cake and even white bread. Outside stood a queue of people, purses full of money, waiting to buy at fantastic prices. She thought of the millions of starving workers, the needy elderly and the rickety children in Russia. What would they think of the Revolution if they saw this display? She hurried to the Kremlin and told Lenin: "Now as before the workers will say, those who have means can get everything, even white bread and sweets. Fine quality!"

Lenin's face darkened. "You know very well that this was necessary," he said. "We had to make a minor sacrifice to reach a major goal: the consolidation of the important conquests of the Revolution."

Balabanoff was not appeased. Finally Lenin said: "If you have some concrete proposal, write to me." She wrote Lenin a long letter. But there was no answer.

Soup kitchens were opened up along the railroad lines.

CHAPTER 19

Kasimir Malevich, Suprematist Composition, 1914.

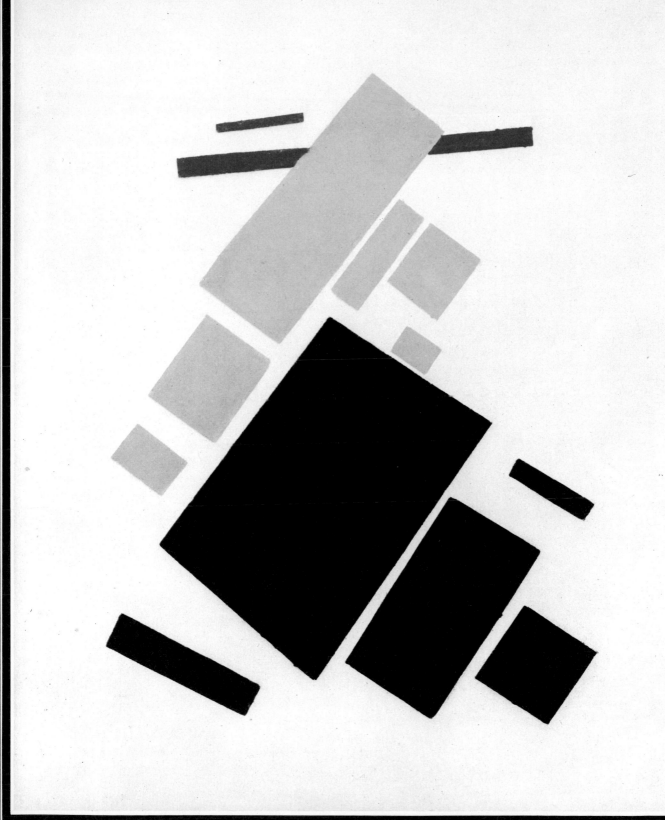

There was hardly a day when Lenin did not address a committee, a plenum, a soviet or a congress. Here he speaks to the Second Congress of the Communist International in 1920.

FACING PAGE
Lenin was informal in his public appearances. He liked to sit on the steps of a

platform or loll in the rear

One day in August, 1921, Victor Serge, a Russian-French anarchist and strong supporter of the Revolution, went to the Art House on the Moika in Petrograd to pay a call on Nikolai Gumilev, a poet and old friend and adversary of his Paris days. Gumilev had been first married to Anna Akhmatova, a daring and beautiful young poet of pre-revolutionary Petersburg, a woman who by the time of her death in 1969 was recognized as the finest Russian poet of the century. The marriage of Akhmatova and Gumilev was brief and stormy. They had one son, Lev, who in the 1930's was to be sent to one of Stalin's prison camps.

In 1921 Gumilev, having served in the Russian Army during World War I, emerged as a romantic monarchist. Now he had a new wife, Olga, a tall young girl with slender neck and frightened eyes. She whispered to Serge that Gumilev had been arrested three days earlier.

Serge went straight to the Petrograd Soviet. The news was true, but Gumilev did not seem to be in great danger; he had written some counter-revolutionary documents but it was hard to take them seriously. He was spending his time reciting his poems to the Chekists. However, Gumilev was soon convicted and the Cheka ordered him shot; one of Serge's friends hurried to Moscow and intervened with Felix Dzerzhinsky, the Cheka chief.

"Are we entitled to shoot one of Russia's two or three poets of the first order?" he asked.

"Are we entitled to make an exception of a poet and still shoot the others?" Dzerzhinsky responded.

And so at dawn on the edge of a forest, Gumilev, his cap pulled over his eyes, a cigarette dangling from his lips, was shot in the name of Lenin's Revolution. He showed the same calm, Serge was told, as he expressed in one of his poems: "And fearless I shall appear before the Lord God."

It was not a good time in Russia for poets. Alexander Blok lay desperately ill. He had been failing for two years, it was not just his body, it was his spirit. In February, just before the Kronstadt days, he had spoken at the Pushkin anniversary: "Calm and freedom are necessary for the release of harmony. Bureaucrats attempt to take them away and to force poetry into artificial channels." He told Korney Chukovsky: "There are no sounds! All sounds have ceased. It is impossible to write under such oppression." On May 26 he wrote to Chukovsky: "I no longer have either soul or body. I am sick as I have never been before. Dirty rotten Mother Russia has devoured me as a sow gobbles up her sucking pig."

Three days later Gorky was urgently urging Commissar Lunacharsky to send Blok to Finland for treatment. Nothing was done. In July Gorky again sought to get help for Blok, he was suffering from scurvy, asthmatic attacks and had fallen into extreme depression and delirium. On August 20 Blok died. There were those who said Blok's fate proved the validity of his poem, "The Twelve". Blind elemental peasant anarchy was, indeed, devouring Russia's genius as a sow does its offspring.

So was determined the fate of the one man whose imagination, better than any other's, captured the essence of the Revolution. It was one tragedy among many.

On September 30 Alexander Berkman sat on a familiar bench in the Alexandrovsky Gardens beside the Kremlin walls. He had last sat there with Fanya Baron, a bright, idealist anarchist with a silvery laugh. He had been afraid for her safety, anarchists were being rounded up everywhere. She reassured him that no one would recognize her, disguised as a peasant. Now she was dead, shot by the Cheka in Odessa along with Lev Chorny, a poet and theoritician of the anarchist movement whom Serge had known in the days when both used to stroll in the Luxembourg Gardens of Paris. Why had they died? Berkman could not understand. The Cheka called them bandits. Emma Goldman wanted to chain herself to a railing at the Third Congress of the International and shout out a protest. She was persuaded not to speak; such words would not move Lenin or Zinoviev.

One small forum of artistic thought managed to stay alive, the Free Philosophical Society, in which Andrei Bely and Ivanov-Razumnik were active. Its tiny meetings were held in Bely's vast room in the General Staff Building, just above the police offices.

There is death-like quality to the faces of these peasants who plied their cannibalistic trade among the starving and half-dead.

FACING PAGE
A young commissar stolidly jots down details of these dealers in human flesh. Their eyes stare in emptiness.

246

Bely, like Blok, had been a supporter of the Bolsheviks. Now he had begun to wonder.

"What can I do now in this life?" he asked. "I cannot live outside this Russia of ours and I cannot breathe within it."

Serge sought to reassure him. But he himself was beginning to have doubts. Soon the police dissolved the Free Philosophical Society.

Ivan Bunin had long since left Russia to make his home for the rest of his life in France. Dmitri Merzhkovsky and his wife Zinaida Gippius followed in his path. Leonid Andreyev was dead. Mayakovsky was still the Revolution's darling, but hardly Lenin's. When he heard that 50,000 copies of Mayakovsky's poem "150 Million"(later much praised by Stalin) were being printed he sent a note to Lunacharsky: "This is absurd, stupid, monstrously stupid and pretentious. In my opinion only one in ten of such pieces should be printed and not more than 1,500 copies for libraries and eccentrics. And Lunacharsky should be whipped for futurism." The poet Khlebnikov was dead. The poetess Marina Tsvetaeva was emigrating (ultimately she would return to Stalin's Russia and kill herself). There was a rumor (untrue) that Akhmatova had committed suicide on hearing the news of Gumilev's execution.

And soon Gorky would leave Russia. Since his reconciliation with Lenin he had been acting as the Revolution's conscience — in so far as it had one. He it was who wrote, called or telegraphed Lenin with urgent pleas that an injustice be rectified, that a Grand Duke not be shot as a hostage (usually it turned out that these requests were received too late), that a starving poet be given food, that a freezing artist's family be afforded shelter, that an ageing scientist be permitted to go abroad for treatment, that a harmless bourgeois widow be allowed to join her children in Paris.

"If we survived those breadless, typhoidal years," Korney Chukovsky recalled, "we owe it in large measure to our 'kinship' with Maxim Gorky, to whom all of us, great and small, became in those days a kindred family."

Once Gorky got the young poet Vsevelod Ivanov paper on which to write his poems. Also a room in which to live and a pair of boots.

As 1921 wore on Gorky's ability to help grew weaker. The wife of Lev Kamenev (the Party boss in Moscow) didn't like Gorky's wife, the actress Andreyeva. Madame Kameneva controlled the Russian theater. The brooding theatrical director Meyerhold supported Kameneva. Gorky himself could not abide Zinoviev, the Petrograd boss. With the two big city party bosses against him Gorky found his influence with Lenin dwindling.

After Kronstadt some surviving sailors made their way to Gorky and told him of the wholesale executions being carried out by Zinoviev, also that Zinoviev had provoked the uprising. Gorky took the story to Lenin, and Lenin reprimanded Zinoviev. The feud between Zinoviev and Gorky grew more bitter.

Finally, Lenin began to urge Gorky to leave Russia "for reasons of health". Gorky did, but not without performing one more remarkable service for his country. Russia was starving to death, even Lenin admitted that not since 1891 had there been anything like it. Actually it was far worse than the Volga famine of the 1890's. The American Relief Administration had offered aid to Russia, but it had been loftily rejected. Now Lenin had to have it if the country was to survive. People were eating clay and twigs in the villages. Cannibalism had appeared. Typhus and cholera were rampant.

On July 23, 1921 Gorky's message went out "To All Honest People".

"The grain-growing steppes are smitten by crop failure," Gorky wrote. "Russia's misfortune offers humanitarians a splendid opportunity to demonstrate the vitality of humanitarianism. Give bread and medicine."

There was an immediate reply from Herbert Hoover. Aid was almost immediately on the way — 800,000 tons of food. The Americans fed almost every child in Petrograd. Food trains penetrated the depths of the Ukraine and the Tambov. Millions of Russian lives were saved and even forty years later Americans travelling through those areas encountered Russians who expressed quiet thanks for the American help (long since denigrated by Soviet propaganda organs as a US effort to use "food as a weapon").

In September Gorky left Russia — whether for reasons of health or politics is still not known. He would not return for a decade.

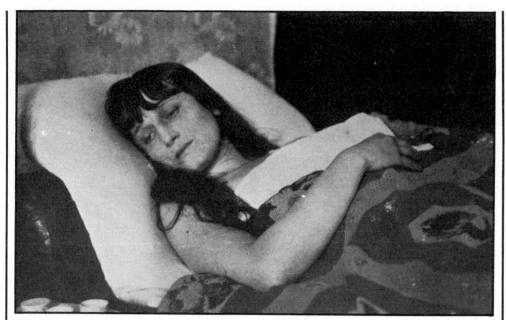

The millstones of the Revolution ground hard. In a world of destruction, of arbitrary dictatorship, of contending bureaucrats the writers were not the only victims. In art, lines began to be drawn. Chagall had been named director of the School of Art in his native Vitebsk but Malevich took the post away from him and Chagall returned in anger to Moscow. He worked for a while as a scenic designer for the State Jewish Theater, decorating the entrance of the theater with a frieze which was later destroyed when the theater was closed in one of Stalin's anti-semitic campaigns. Chagall made his way to Paris. Olga Rosanova died. Kandinsky went to the Bauhaus. Lissitsky also went to Germany. The Pevsner brothers, Anton and Naum (better known under the name of Gabo which he later gave himself) departed, Anton to France, Gabo to Berlin, to London and finally to America.

Sharper and sharper divisions emerged. Malevich, Kandinsky and the Pevsners had stood for the concept of art as a spiritual activity, designed to enhance man's vision of the world. Tatlin and Rodchenko violently opposed them. Art was a functional process, the artist a kind of mechanic or technician of the brush or chisel. Tatlin and Rodchenko prevailed – for a while.

The first signs had begun to appear that the Revolution was not going to be the boundlessly creative environment which Russia's artists had envisaged.

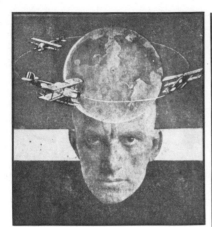

If the Revolution had a
house poet surely it was
Vladimir Mayakovsky. It
was, he said, his Revolution.
He walked into it and started
opening windows. No one
was more at home.
Whatever was happening,
wherever it was,
Mayakovsky was there with
his polemic verse, his
irrespressible spirit, his quick
pen and brush. He created
cartoon windows for
ROSTA, the Russian
Telegraph Agency, to plug
whatever propaganda cause
was going. He celebrated the
Revolution's triumphs in epic
poems. He fought with his
fellow poets and artists. He
engaged in mad love affairs.
He wrote plays and staged
pageants. He decorated
propaganda trains and
invented new art forms. Not
everyone liked him. Lenin
thought he was brash and his
verse in bad taste. His career
rocketed to heights and sank
into pits. In the end he killed
himself and then, as
Pasternak was to say, Stalin
sold him to the Russian
people as Catherine II had
sold the peasants Irish
potatoes.

Mayakovsky and his circle.
He stands to rear. Next to
him Osip Brik, husband of
the love of Mayakovsky's
life, and Boris Pasternak.
Sitting, Elsa Triolet and
Lila Brik.

Mayakovsky towering over Sergei Eisenstein, the film director, Elsa Triolet and Lily Brik.

Caricature by Mayakovsky of the White Russian General Denikin, dated 1920.

Sergei Eisenstein, top, sits in the Tsar's throne on the Winter Palace set of October: Ten Days That Shook the World.

RIGHT
Eisenstein directs the camera in the shooting of the attack on the Winter Palace scene for October.

Following pages:

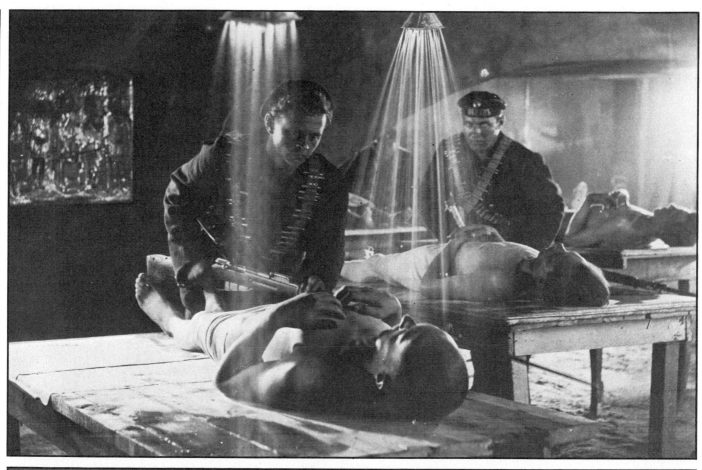

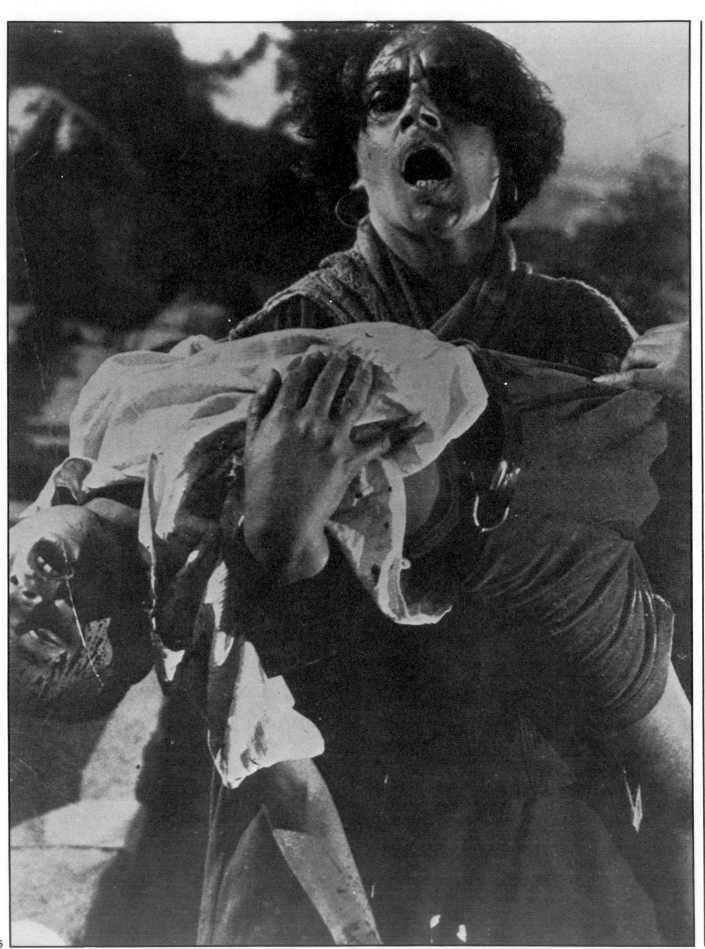

CHAPTER 20

The Bolsheviks utilized May Day to carry their revolutionary message to the world. Here the workers of the world are reminded of Karl Marx's call that they "have nothing to lose but their chains.

1 МАЯ.
РАБОЧИМ НЕЧЕГО ТЕРЯТЬ, КРОМЕ СВОИХ ЦЕПЕЙ;
А ПРИОБРЕТУТ ОНИ ЦЕЛЫЙ МИР.

К. Маркс и Ф. Энгельс.

Lenin watching a troop review from the back of a truck.

n August of 1921 Lenin fell ill. Nothing serious apparently. Probably pure overwork. But he took a vacation, did a little light reading, including a French adventure story, *Les Exploits de Rocambole,* which had to be retrieved from the Lubyanka prison where it was being enjoyed by several prominent Menshevik and Socialist Revolutionary prisoners. He cut down on his writing — but not a great deal.

Lenin had been running full tilt since November 7, 1917. He was tired and frequently irritable. Some Mensheviks thought that the brief illness in August, 1921, marked his first small stroke. This is unlikely, but it may have been a warning sign of symptoms to come.

Four years had taken its toll of Lenin, of his Party, of Russia and its people. Political reputations had risen and fallen. Trotsky stood as Lenin's only real equal but he had won no great following within the tight Bolshevik circle, a circle composed of stubborn revolutionary members who had demonstrated their Party conformity and bureaucratic skills long before 1917.

Within this narrow coterie the bosses of Moscow and Petrograd, Kamenev and Zinoviev, towered over the others. They might be unpleasant individuals; Balabanoff might regard them as moral cretins; but Lenin trusted them to get the work done. He also had come to trust his Georgian lieutenant, Josef Stalin, the Party's Secretary and very clearly a man on the make. But Lenin's trust in Stalin had its limits. Stalin was not a pleasant man. He was hard to get on with and when, for example, Lenin's old benefactress, Fofanova, came to see what Lenin thought of a proposal that she go to work for Stalin, Lenin recommended against it. He didn't think she would get on with Stalin, the job might turn out badly, he thought she should find work elsewhere.

There were many things on Lenin's mind in that autumn of 1921. He found time to rage about the Kremlin elevator service. The elevators were sometimes not working for three days at a time. This was "utterly scandalous". What about people with bad hearts? He ordered punishment for those responsible. He was trying wildly — there is no other word for it — to find solutions to the economic quagmire into which Russia had fallen. Every kind of note flooded from his office. A proposal to get a young American named Armand Hammer interested in electrifying the Urals. An appeal to get coal workers to come back to the Donets basin by offering them extra food. A note to Trotsky worrying about money to pay the new commercial concessionaires. ("The wail about the lack of money is general and universal. We could very well blow up.")

But, everlastingly, his notes, his attention, his concern was drawn to the persistent, glacial, irresistible spread of sloth, bureaucracy and what the Russians call *poshlost,* grinding mediocrity, which like a grey sludge was burying the new Revolution in the mores of old Russia.

The institution which had been set up to try to correct this situation was Rabkrin, the Workers-Peasants Inspection, headed by Stalin. Lenin regarded Stalin as a man who got things done. But now he was beginning to wonder. Perhaps the first evidence of Lenin's emerging doubt about Stalin was a long memorandum in late September 1921 about the work of Rabkrin. It said, essentially, that instead of correcting conditions, Rabkrin had become part of the problem. "The task of Rabkrin," wrote Lenin, "is not even and not only the task of 'catching' or 'convicting' (that is the task of the courts) but of timely and competent correction." Stalin whipped off an immediate reply to Lenin, shifting the guilt to his subordinates. There were to be more of these memoranda as Lenin grew more and more preoccupied with the question of what was going wrong with his Revolution.

Day by day, week by week and month by month this question would possess him and he would die without putting his finger on where the trouble lay or devising a plan to defeat it.

In fact the Party machinery was badly worn by four years of crisis. It had been a one-man operation in the pre-Revolution days. Lenin never permitted any other kind of organization. But the seeds of trouble had been apparent since the outbreak of the February Revolution. It was no accident that, from the start, there had been a split between Lenin in Switzerland and the Communist exiles from Siberia — Stalin, Zinoviev, Kamenev and the rest who took over the Party and ran it before Lenin's return from Zurich. Inevitably, the men at home felt they had a better grasp on affairs than the man abroad. They had disagreed with Lenin's analysis, they had edited his communications, suppressed some and published a few in shortened versions. Lenin was much more radical, more revolutionary, than they were.

The split was patched over and Lenin had managed to win back control of the Party after returning in April 1917, but it was a patch which did not endure. Each crisis strained the stitches. When Lenin went into hiding in Finland in the summer of 1917 and Stalin took charge in Petrograd, it was clear the two men had different views. When autumn came and Lenin frantically urged his colleagues that the time was ripe for a *coup d'état* the split appeared again. Trotsky, Lenin's great recruit to bolshevism, played his own hand but it was usually closer to Lenin than to the Siberian trio.

In the triumph of October the Bolsheviks came together again, but within days they had split and split again, some members resigning and being reinstated almost too rapidly for recording. Lenin carried the day by force of his personality and intellect but the inner Party circle was far from unanimous.

During the terrible and continuous crises of 1917-21, lines of cleavage and signs of political ambition emerged. Zinoviev took over Petrograd as his fief; Kamenev had Moscow; Trotsky had the Red Army; Stalin the Party apparatus. Stalin's position was least conspicuous (his effort to win military kudos during the Civil War had been no great success, although later he would make much of his fighting at Tsaritsyn).

Stalin was not widely known to the public. He was not popular with his comrades and had not been since the old Siberian days. His manner was rude and most of the Europeanized Party leaders who had spent long periods of exile in the West, looked down on him as a narrow, provincial and uncultured man. They snubbed and slighted him. He would not forget.

Stalin's attitude toward Lenin was ambivalent. As a young revolutionary he had chosen Lenin as his leader. His first sight of him (at Tammerfors during the 1905 Revolution) had been disappointing. Lenin was not the grandiose figure he imagined. Close reading of Stalin's correspondence, his speeches at Party meetings, his voting in Party sessions, the memoirs of those who knew him, make it possible to trace a dichotomy in Stalin. He supported Lenin on major questions but when not in Lenin's presence he often made disparaging remarks about *starik,* the old man.

By early 1922 Stalin had clearly emerged as the principal bureaucrat in the Soviet apparatus and, equally clearly, Lenin had begun to center his attention on him. He began to set up a new apparatus, designed to replace Stalin's Rabkrin, and he had picked two trusted Bolsheviks, Tsurupa and Rykov, to try to shake the bureaucracy (and possibly Stalin) out of the system. In February of 1922 he wrote Tsurupa in the bluntest language employing obscenities which he rarely used in correspondence. "We do not need a 'department for international trade'," he raged. "We have enough of such shit as *departments*. . . .We are being sucked into a foul bureaucratic swamp. . . .You must free yourself from the turmoil and disorder which *is driving us all crazy.*"

And finally he exploded: "All disorders and decisions are dirty pieces of paper. Institutions — are shit. Decrees — are shit. In writing decrees and orders we are stupid to the point of idiocy. The selection of people and the verification of results — that's the whole point."

Lenin was ill again that winter. In letter after letter, note after note, he excused himself from meetings and problems. He suffered from insomnia and splitting headaches. His doctors insisted that he get rest and he began to spend more time at the old Morozov estate just out of town, keeping in touch by telephone, notes and memoranda. Despite his quarrels and suspicions, Lenin approved the appointment of Stalin as General Secretary of the Party; at the same time he offered Trotsky the post of Deputy Chairman of the Soviet of People's Commissars — that is, his own first deputy. Trotsky declined.

Lenin also took the time to insist on the adoption in the Soviet criminal code of a merciless affirmation of the right of the State to invoke terror, "to legalize it as a principle, plainly without any make-believe or embellishment. It must be formulated in the broadest possible manner." This was done, and together with the ban on dissidence within the Party, which Lenin had rammed through a year earlier, gave Lenin's

Lenin records one of his speeches on an Edison phonograph recorder.

successor the weapons with which he would mercilessly purge, imprison, kill and torture millions of Russian citizens including almost every old Bolshevik who had stood close to Lenin, not excluding Lenin's wife and immediate family.

Lenin was examined several times during the spring of 1922 by physicians. German specialists were flown in. One of the bullets that had remained in his neck after Kaplan's assassination attempt was removed and the doctors found nothing wrong with him except the results of years of overwork.

But at 10 am on May 26, 1922 Lenin's sister Maria telephoned to the chief Kremlin physician, Dr Rozanov, from the Morozov villa. Lenin was ill. He had stomach pains and was vomiting, his head ached. He had suffered a slight stroke, the physicians found. There was partial paralysis of the right side, a slight slurring of speech. He was alert and in relatively good humor but he did not minimize the seriousness of his illness. "This is the first bell," he said.

He followed his regime of rest and light exercise faithfully. And he took great interest in a show trial — the first of the Soviet regime staged in Moscow in which thirty-four surviving Socialist Revolutionary leaders were convicted of treason. All Europe watched the trial as well, and almost every prominent left-wing writer and political figure denounced the procedure. Perhaps that is why although twelve Socialist Revolutionaries including the well-known Abram Gotz, Yevgenia Timofeev and Lev J. Gershtein, were given death sentences the penalties were not carried out. Not just then. The Socialist Revolutionaries were sent into the growing Soviet prison system, there to linger until Stalin got around to executing them in the 1930's.

As summer passed Lenin's strength returned, and he went back to the preoccupations of winter and spring — bureaucracy and Stalin. Stalin had visited Lenin at the Morozov villa, had had his picture taken, had given interviews to the newspapers. His stature was growing.

Now Lenin had a new quarrel with Stalin, this one over what he regarded as Stalin's chauvinistic attitude toward the smaller Soviet nationalities, particularly those of Stalin's own Caucasus. Stalin, in Lenin's opinion, was more Russian than the Russians and he proposed to correct this.

The issue was joined over the draft of a new Soviet Constitution. Lenin wanted a federation of republics, Stalin wanted a plain subordination. And for the first time (so far as is yet known) Stalin revealed on paper his *grubost,* his rudeness, to Lenin. He accepted Lenin's viewpoint but, as Lenin's Soviet biographers report (the text of the letter has not yet been published), "in an intolerably rude manner", and he made it plain that his submission to Lenin was merely formal. When Lev Kamenev told Stalin that "Lenin is prepared to go to war on the issue of independence," Stalin replied: "In my opinion it is necessary to be firm against Ilyich."

Lenin, suffering from a toothache, gave his reply in a note to the Politburo: "I declare war to the death on Great Russian chauvinism. I shall eat it with all my healthy teeth as soon as I get rid of this damned tooth."

So the situation simmered during the autumn of 1922 as Lenin gradually moved back into the center of Party affairs, shaking off his illness. But his preoccupation with what he saw as the failures of the Revolution did not evaporate. He continued to try to find a cure for the incurable — and intensified his concern over what came to be called the "Georgian" question, that is, what Lenin saw as the chauvinistic, Great Russian, attitude of Stalin and several of his henchmen toward Georgia and the Caucasus.

By December Lenin's health was again deteriorating. He tried to run things as of old but could not. On December 13 he suffered a second cerebral thrombosis. It came after an agitated discussion with Felix Dzerzhinsky, the Cheka chief, on the Georgian question. Dzerzhinsky was supporting Stalin. On the 13th Lenin saw Stalin for two hours, almost certainly it was an unpleasant conversation. Did Stalin deliberately provoke Lenin? Did he, knowing Lenin's fragile state of health and the growing danger of Lenin's opposition to him personally, try to speed matters a bit by playing on Lenin's nerves? The answer will probably never be known, but enough has been revealed of Stalin's preoccupation with medical means of eliminating people from his path to make the question more than academic.

What is known, is that Lenin now began to face up to the possibility of death or

This poster by D. Moor is called A Red Present for the White Pans, *the white noblemen opposing the Bolshevik regime.*

КРАСНЫЙ ПОДАРОК
БЕЛОМУ ПАНУ

ДВИНЬ-КА
ЭТИМ ЧЕМОДАН-
ЧИКОМ ПАНА В ЛОБ

Stalin's mother, Ekaterina Djugashvili, was the strongest influence on his early days.

RIGHT TOP
Stalin was arrested for the first time on the night of April 5, 1902 in a police raid on the headquarters of the Batum Social Democratic Committee. He was held in prison for about eighteen months before being exiled to a Siberian village named Novaia Uda in Irkutsk province. In this photo Stalin, marked with an X, is said to be starting his long journey into exile.

RIGHT BOTTOM
Stalin is depicted here in Siberian exile.

FACING PAGE
One of the earliest surviving photographs of Iosif Djugashvili (Josef Stalin). This portrait was taken in 1900 when Stalin, a young ecclesiastical school student, was just beginning his revolutionary career.

total disablement. As rapidly as possible, he sought to put his affairs in order. Despite his physical condition, he insisted on meeting his secretaries and dictating a series of notes and articles. He met — even if very briefly — with a few key individuals; and he deliberately sought to draw Trotsky to his side, to shift on to him the burden of defending his policies; and he fought, as never before, to block Stalin. He thought he was succeeding and wrote in triumph to Trotsky "Comrade Trotsky: It seems we succeeded in taking the position without a single shot by a simple maneuver. I propose that we do not stop and continue the attack."

But Lenin's pleasure was premature. Stalin was not to be thwarted by a half-paralyzed man, even if his name was Lenin. Stalin telephoned Krupskaya and up-braided her for helping Lenin engage in Party affairs against the dictate of the doctors. He threatened to bring her up on charges. Krupskaya in anguish appealed to Lev Kamenev for support. "During all these thirty years I have never heard from any comrade one word of rudeness...I am a living person and my nerves are strained to the utmost."

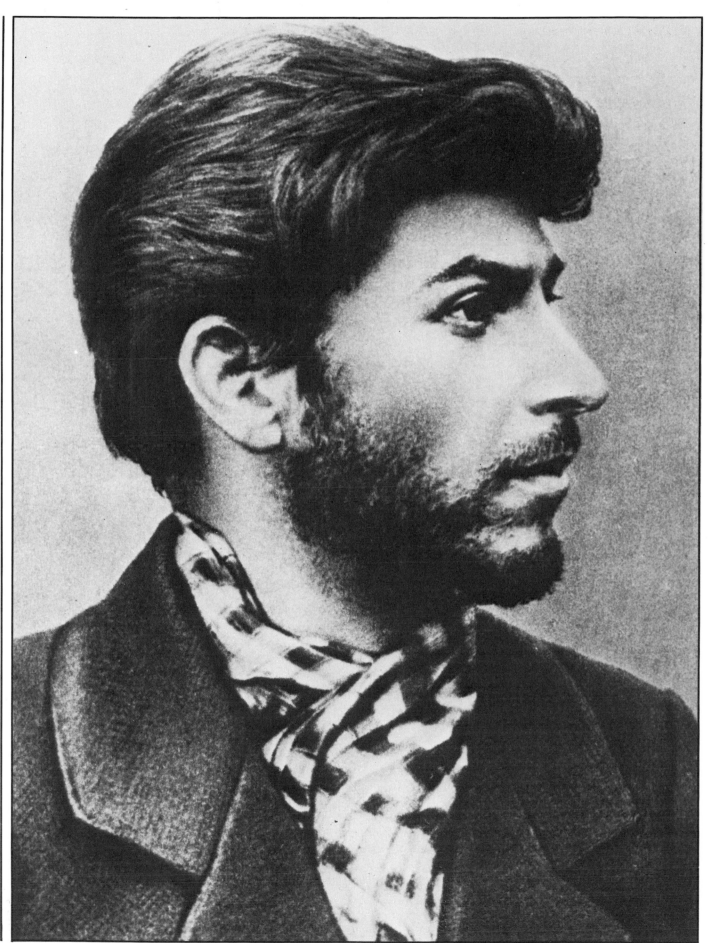

Stalin, Lenin, Kalinin.

Despite his illness Lenin began to dictate – and he would continue this over a period of nearly two weeks – what came to be known as his "last testament". It was a series of instructions to his Party on what to do once he was gone. He characterized all of the leaders. He warned of a coming split between Stalin and Trotsky. Stalin, he said, had accumulated "boundless power" and it was not certain that he would use it with sufficient caution. Trotsky was "the most able person" on the Central Committee but had too much self-confidence. He recalled that Zinoviev and Kamenev had opposed the October coup and singled out Nikolai Bukharin as the most valuable and distinguished theoretician of the Party. Pyatakov he thought too authoritarian. On January 4, 1923, perhaps having heard something about Stalin's rudeness to Krupskaya, he added a postscript:

> Stalin is too rude and this fault quite tolerable in the company of Communists and among us becomes intolerable for one who holds the office of General Secretary. Therefore I propose to the comrades to consider a means of removing Stalin from that post and appoint another person to this position who in all respects differs from Stalin only in superiority, namely, more patient, more loyal, more polite, and more attentive to comrades, less capricious, and so forth.

> This circumstance may seem to be an insignificant trifle. But I think from the point of view of the relationship between Stalin and Trotsky which I discuss above this is not a trifle, or is a trifle which may acquire decisive significance.

Lenin's health began to improve and he managed to dictate a series of articles on subjects dear to his heart – plans for reorganizing the government and finally one on the Workers-Peasant Inspection. Each article was dutifully published but, when it came to the final article, Stalin opposed publication (it was of course a bullet aimed at his heart). V. V. Kuibyshev proposed that it be printed in a single edition of *Pravda* to be delivered only to Lenin. But, in the end, it came out in Pravda on March 4, 1923.

On the next day Lenin dictated to his secretary Volodicheva this note:

> To Comrade Stalin:
> Copies for Kamenev and Zinoviev:
> Dear Comrade Stalin!
> You permitted yourself a rude summons of my wife on the telephone and you went on to reprimand her rudely. Despite the fact that she told you she agreed to

forget what was said, nevertheless, Zinoviev and Kamenev heard about it from her. I have no intention of forgetting so easily something which has been done against me, and I do not have to stress that I consider anything done against my wife as done against me. I am therefore asking you to weigh carefully whether you agree to retract your words and apolgize, or whether you prefer the severance of relations between us.

Sincerely,
Lenin.

Why Lenin waited until March to call Stalin to responsibility for the rudeness to Krupskaya which occurred in December is not known, possibly there had been a new incident.

Late that day Lenin dictated a note to Trotsky asking him to take up the defense of the "Georgian case" because he could not trust the judgment of Stalin and Dzerzhinsky. On March 6 he sent a note to the Georgians, Mdivani and Makharadze, declaring that "Orzhonikidze's brutality [in handling the Georgians] and the connivance of Stalin and Dzerzhinsky have outraged me."

On the 7th the note to Stalin was delivered — Krupskaya had tried to persuade the secretaries not to send it. Stalin immediately wrote out a note of apology which was returned, it is said, to Krupskaya. The note has never been published nor does Lenin seem to have seen it. His health was deteriorating disastrously, and on March 9 he suffered a massive stroke which took away his power of speech and completely paralyzed him.

Lenin's career had come to an end; his Revolution was running on a course he had never set, with a man whom he had come to abhor moving to the helm.

Lenin lived on for nearly a year. In late autumn and early winter his health had begun to improve. He could walk and read and indicate his wishes. He had even paid one nostalgic visit to his old Kremlin quarters. On January 7, Christmas by the Russian Orthodox calendar, he had one last celebration a Christmas tree and presents for the children at the Morozov villa.

Then, on January 21, 1924, he died. Trotsky was ill and recuperating in the Caucasus. He did not return for the funeral. Peasants and workers from all parts of Russia made their way to Moscow for the ceremony on January 26, and the lying-in-state of the body in the Hall of Columns, once the Nobleman's Club. Stalin was the principal funeral orator and in his old ecclesiastical school style he turned the speech

Stalin and his close colleagues of the early 1930's — Kalinin, Lazar Kaganovich, Sergo Orzhonikidze and Klimenti Voroshilov.

into a kind of orthodox ritual: "We vow to thee, Comrade Lenin, that we will honorably fulfill this thy commandment."

Lenin's body was placed in a mausoleum hastily constructed before the Kremlin wall in Red Square. It was designed by Alexei Shchusev, a leader of the Russian Constructivists and it was to be the only monument in Russia to this remarkably gifted movement which in all other civilized countries was hailed as the advance guard of progress.

Because of the need for haste, the mausoleum was constructed of wood and painted a dull red. Later, the wooden structure was replaced by the red granite and porphyry which still stands as a monument to Lenin and his times. The man who appeared most often on its summit, reviewing parade after parade, demonstrations and reviews over the years, while almost all of his colleagues of 1924 vanished, either by natural death or thanks to his paranoid executions and the vast prison apparatus which he created, was Stalin.

The constructivist artists were scattered to the winds, and by 1932 Stalin's grey and somber cliché, Socialist Realism, reigned as the official artistic creed of his regime – dusty, servile, sterile, bureaucratic, the artistic equivalent of that earthy epithet which Lenin had hurled at Stalin in his final anger.

RIGHT AND OVERLEAF
Lenin suffered his first stroke in June 1922 and his health took a downward course. He recovered enough to return to work in autumn 1922 but in December suffered more strokes. He managed to continue dictating for a few weeks and composed his so-called 'Last Testament' warning the Party against Stalin. Then in March 1923 he suffered a stroke which left him speechless. He was an invalid unable to communicate more than simple expressions until his death on January 21, 1924. He died at an estate just outside Moscow. His body was brought to the Hall of Columns, the former Club of Nobles, where it lay in state.

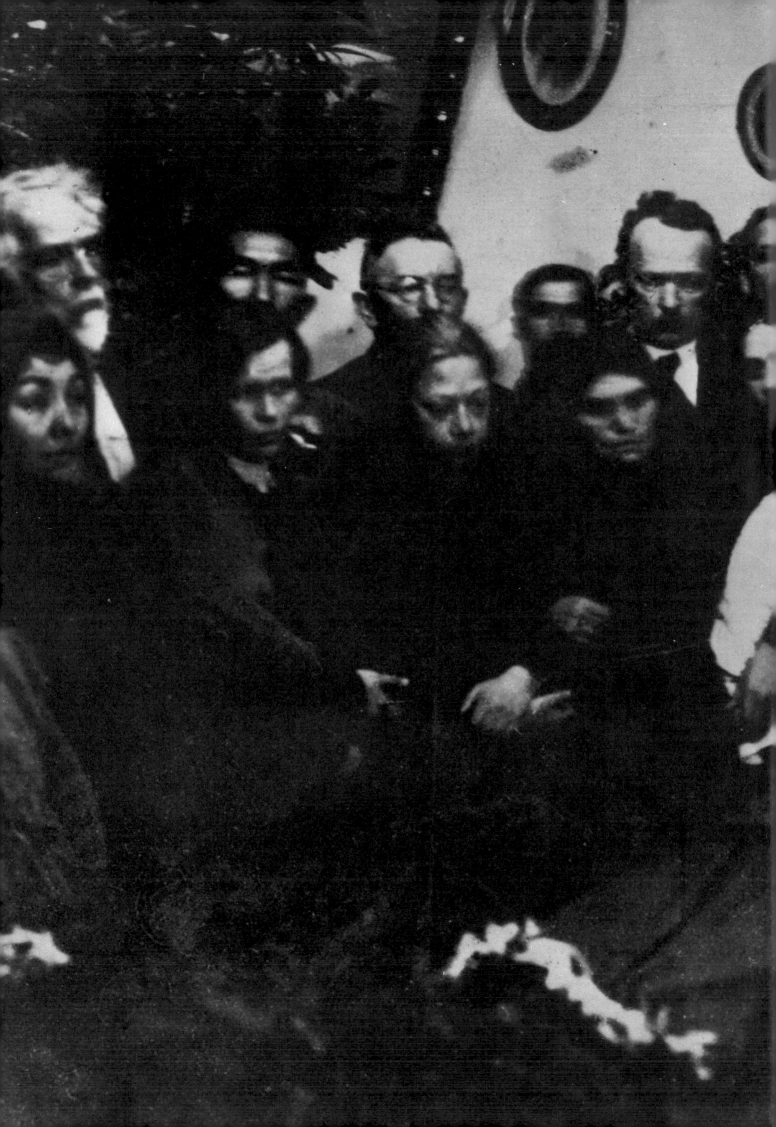

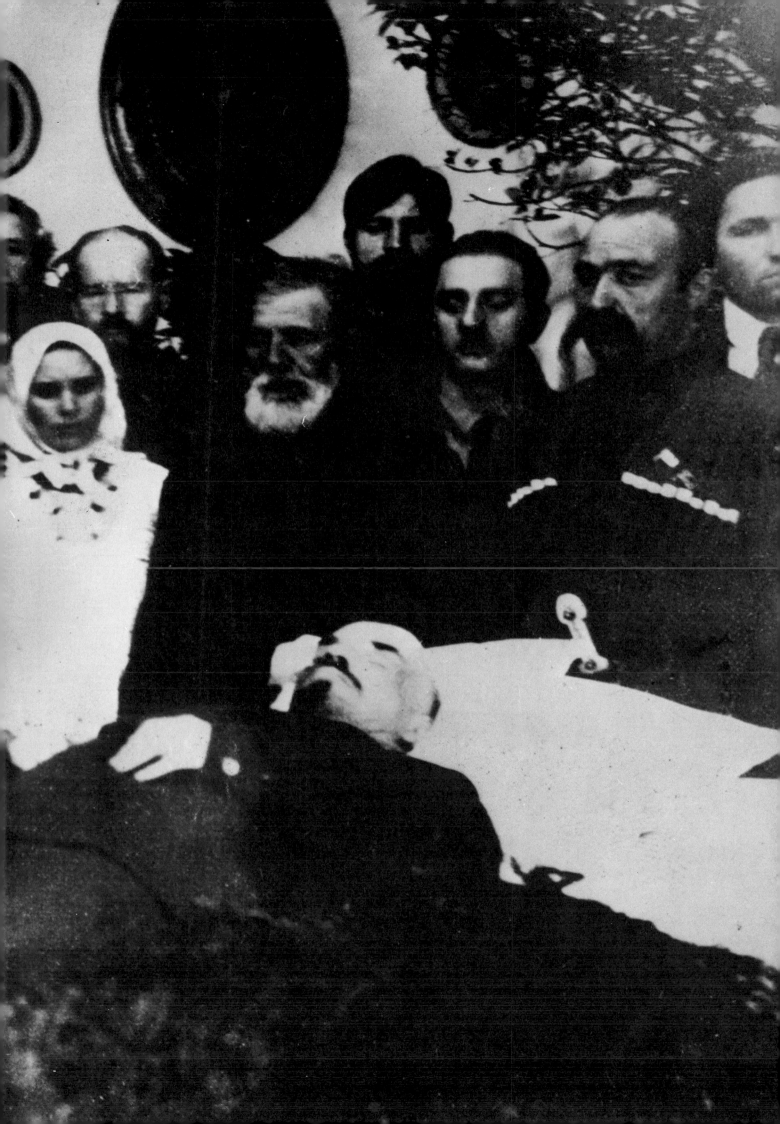

CHAPTER 21

A late example of El Lissitsky's Constructivist poster art. This was designed for a Russian gravure exhibition in Zurich in 1929.

Every possible means of
propaganda and force was
mobilized by Stalin for his
campaign to "collectivize"
Russian farmland, crush the
Kulaks, *the rich peasants, and
industrialize Russia. Above, a
postcard; at right a montage.*

FACING PAGE
*Postcard celebrated the Stalin
Five-Year-Plan for industry.
Stalin's great breakthrough
came in 1929 when, his
dictatorial power assured, he
launched the first Five-Year-
Plan in industry and started
the collectivization of
agriculture. The Five-Year-
Plan was to be the first of
many designed to raise Soviet
industrial levels to those of the
West. The agricultural
program was designed to end
private farming and assemble
all of Russia's peasants in
collective or state farming
enterprises. The agricultural
program was carried out with
swiftness and cruelty.
Millions of peasants were
displaced, and millions were
killed or died of deprivation
and starvation.*

enin was gone. At first that seemed to be the big change.
Mayakovsky spent eight months writing a poem. "Vladimir Ilyich
Lenin", and when he finally read it at the Press House, on October
18 1924, someone said it should be called "I and Lenin". Mayakovsky
retorted: "My poem 'Lenin' is a genuine epic."

Russia still seemed crowded with artistic genius – Boris Pasternak,
Lila Brik, Mayakovsky's great love, her husband Osip Brik, Burlyuk (but he was soon
to leave), Rodchenko, Popova. Le Corbusier would be invited to put up one of his
finest buildings (now a shabby ruin); the magazine LEF, with Mayakovsky as its
brightest spirit and Rodchenko to devise its illustrations, illuminated the scene. Sergei
Eisenstein had begun his film epics; *Battleship Potemkin* lay ahead, so did *Ivan the
Terrible* and Stalin's fateful intervention. Mary Pickford and Douglas Fairbanks came
to Moscow. Fairbanks posed in the wide-mouthed Ivan the Great cannon on the
Kremlin grounds. Mayakovsky made a tour of America and the constructivists, unable
to get building commissions in Moscow, went to work for the brilliant new theater
directors Vsevelod Meyerhold (who was arrested and died in a concentration camp in
the 1930's, his wife, Zinaida Raikh, murdered by robbers, or plainclothesmen, in their
Moscow apartment) and Tairov, whose Kamerny theater was headed for Stalin's scrap-
heap. Sergei Tretyakov startled the world with his *Roar, China.* (He would die in
Stalin's execution chambers in 1938.)

True, there were tragedies. Sergei Yesenin, Russia's great peasant poet came to the
end of his tether. He had done everything. He had married Isadora Duncan and

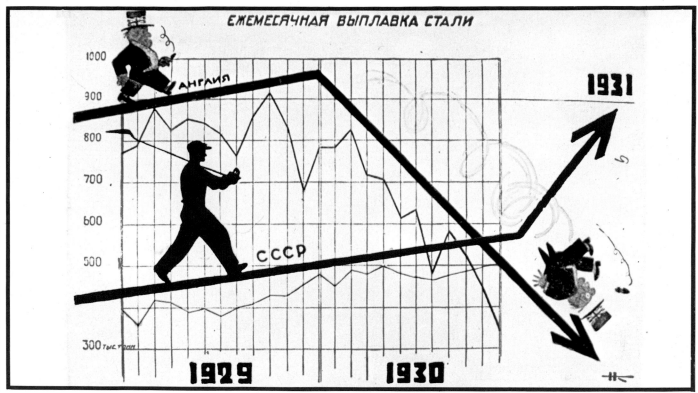

ЕЖЕМЕСЯЧНАЯ ВЫПЛАВКА СТАЛИ

travelled with her to Paris and New York. He had drunk himself into a stupor more times than anyone could count. He had tried drugs, emerged from nervous breakdowns, fallen into hallucinations. He had even returned to his native village but he found nothing there. "What a country!" he exclaimed. "Why in hell did I caterwaul about my being a friend of the people? They have no need of me."

During the Christmas holiday, on December 27, 1925, he wrote a last poem: "To die is not new — but neither is it new to be alive." Then he slashed his wrists and hanged himself in his room at the Angleterre Hotel in what was now Leningrad.

Yesenin's death was, Mayakovsky agreed, a tragedy. He blamed himself. He and his friends had talked of doing something about Yesenin but, as he sadly conceded, nothing was done.

So life went on. On the political front, Stalin easily bested his rivals. He used Kamenev and Zinoviev to drive Trotsky out of the Party, and by 1928 Trotsky was exiled to Alma Ata on the Russian-Chinese frontier and, a year later, expelled to Turkey. He went on to Norway and finally to Mexico. He was the last political opponent Stalin permitted to leave Russia, but in 1940 Stalin's vengeance caught up and Trotsky was assassinated in his Mexico City stronghold.

Once Stalin had dealt with Trotsky he played with his one-time allies as a master angler plays with a trout. He split Zinoviev from Kamenev. He toyed with Bukharin like a child. He pulled the strings of political power into his hands and put his cronies, Budenny and Voroshilov, old cavalrymen from Tsaritsyn days, in higher and higher military posts. He had rid himself of Mikhail Frunze, Trotsky's successor as Red Army chief in 1925, by means of forcing Frunze to undergo an operation which he opposed and from which he died. Boris Pilnyak wrote a *roman à clef* about it called *The Unfinished Moon*. Soon enough Pilnyak would vanish into Stalin's camps and die.

And now, his power secure, Stalin launched the great projects which engraved his mark indelibly on his country's back — the first five-year plan of industrialization, the collectivization of agriculture and the prison labor system.

The first five-year plan, a grandiose scheme for putting Russia into the forefront of the European nations got underway in 1928. It was based, in large measure, on plans which had been drafted as early as 1914 by the Czarist regime. Stalin followed up with a colossal collectivization plan, a blow so staggering to Russian agriculture that, to this day, it has never really recovered. Millions of peasants were displaced. Millions were shot or died of hunger and cold. Famine again swept the country. Appalled at what he

A Russian woman physician conducts stress and fatigue studies with young factory worker.

"At the Bar of Soviet Justice" —
one of the earliest of Stalin's
"show" trials.

had unleashed Stalin backed off a little. But it was only a temporary retreat.

By the late 1920's he had picked up where Lenin left off and had begun to experiment with terror and "show" trials. The first experiment was in 1928, with the so-called Shakhty case in which fifty Russian engineers and three German technicians were charged with sabotaging coal production. This first rehearsal was a bit shaky, the prosecutors and the judges had not yet learned their roles. But by 1930 and the trial of the "Industrial Party" (a non-existent group) the staging and machinery was down pat. Everything was set for the great political melodramas of the mid-1930's in which Stalin would wipe out, first, the old line Bolsheviks, then the military leadership of Marshal Tukhachevsky, and finally begin the delicate process of killing those men he himself had placed in power, meantime providing millions of bodies as labor fodder for the industrial prison camp system.

As the 1920's wound down the future might still be clouded so far as the politicians and analysts were concerned, but it was plain and clear to the creative artists. The literary scene was one of devastation. Gone were the exuberant experimentalists, the avant garde of the early 1920's. Most of the artists had fled abroad. LEF had been silenced. Proletcult was disbanded. RAPP, a new organ of Party political purity, was in the saddle. Mayakovsky was despondent. The Briks were in Paris.

On April 12, 1930 Mayakovsky sat in Herzen House, a writers' club on Tversky Boulevard and talked with the director Alexander Dovzhenko, whose film *Earth* had just been torn to bits by what he called "RAPP cannibal scoundrels and hacks". Mayakovsky said, "Come to me tomorrow, we will see if we cannot bring together a small group for the defense of art because what is happening around us is unbearable, impossible."

Dovzhenko and Mayakovsky didn't manage to meeet on the 13th. The next day at 10.15 am in his room on Lubyansky Pereulok, just behind the great prison of that name, Mayakovsky killed himself with a stage-prop revolver which he had used twelve years before in a film called *Not for Money Born*.

Beside him on a table lay a poem, unfinished:

I am not in a hurry,
        lightnings of cables
                in space
to send,
        will not rouse you from sleep.
As they say,
        a bungled story.

After Mayakovsky's death Josef Stalin issued a statement: "Mayakovsky was and remains the most talented poet of our Soviet epoch. Indifference to his memory and to his work is a crime."

Then began the "selling of Mayakovsky". He was, in Pasternak's words, sold to Russia as Catherine the Great persuaded her peasants to cultivate potatoes.

Stalin had been courting Gorky. His regime must have culture, and Gorky was Russia's greatest cultural monument. Lenin had lost him. Stalin would get him back. In 1928 Gorky came back from Italian exile for a grand tour. It was his sixtieth birthday and he went back to Nizhni Novgorod on the Volga where he was born (soon it would be rechristened Gorky), he went to Tsaritsyn (which was now Stalingrad), to the Caucasus and to Armenia.

He returned in 1929, when he visited the great state farm, Gigant in the Kuban, and Solovki, the worst concentration camp up to that time, sited in an ancient monastery in the Solovetsky islands. He had Cheka men as his guides. The inmates were given new issues of clothing and special rations to feed them up. He wrote a laudatory article about the concentration camp, as later he would edit a collective book about the first great industrial achievement of Soviet slave labor — the White Sea Canal.

The next year Gorky again went back to Russia — to stay until his mysterious death, probably by poison at Stalin's orders, in 1936. He dutifully took his role in Stalin's court, approving Stalin's new definition of the role of writers. Writers, Stalin decreed, "are the engineers of human souls". The blueprints, for these "engineers" was provided, of course, by the man whose name became synonymous with his epoch — Stalin.

FACING PAGE
*Stalin, his daughter Svetlana,
and Sergei Kirov, the
Leningrad Party leader, in
the country.*

The mechanization of agriculture proceeded slowly under the collectivization program but the plan was designed to modernize Soviet farming methods.

RIGHT
This radio tower of Constructivist design was erected in Moscow in the 1920's.

FAR RIGHT
Girl with a jackhammer works on an excavation site.

FACING PAGE
Mayakovsky's literary journal, Novy Lev, featured Constructivist covers, often with industrial subjects.

OVERLEAF
Stalin with Communist Party Congress delegates from Leningrad in 1929.

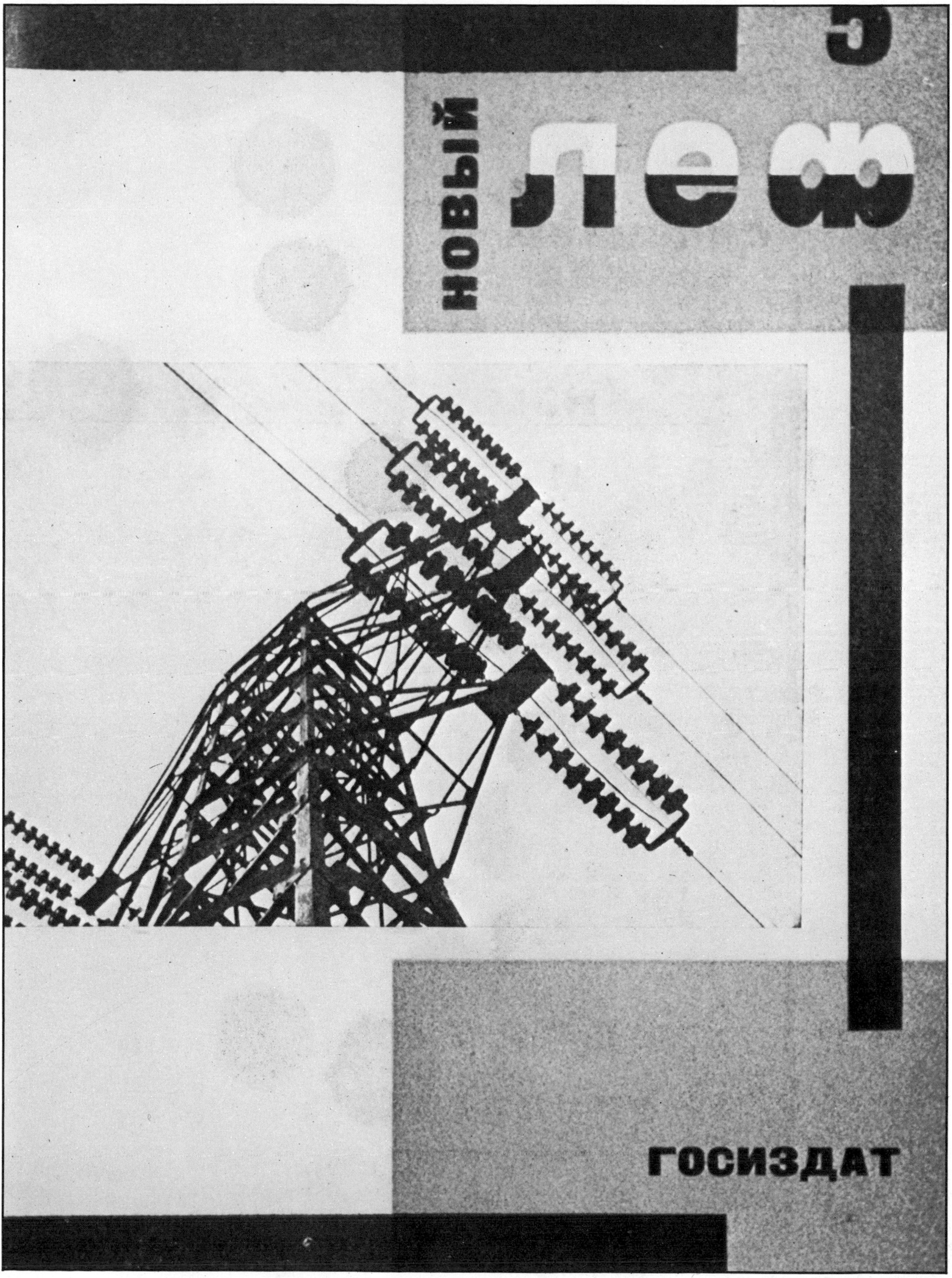
5
НОВЫЙ
леф
ГОСИЗДАТ